D0835856

Mario Reading was brought up in England, Germany, and the South of France. He speaks four languages. He studied Comparative Literature under Malcolm Bradbury and Angus Wilson at the University of East Anglia, where he specialised in French and German literature and translation. During a passionately misspent youth he sold rare books, taught riding in Africa, studied dressage in Vienna, played professional polo in India, Spain and Dubai, helped run his Mexican wife's coffee plantation, and survived a terminal diagnosis for cancer. An award-winning novelist, he is also the author of the highly personal *Dictionary of Cinema* (reissued as *The Movie Companion*), *Nostradamus: The Complete Prophecies for the Future*, and *The Watkins Dictionary of Dreams*.

By the same author

Nostradamus: The Complete Prophecies for the Future

The Watkins Dictionary of Dreams

The Music-Makers

The Movie Companion

NOSTRADAMUS
The Good News

MARIO READING

WATKINS PUBLISHING

LONDON

This edition published in the UK 2007 by
Watkins Publishing, Sixth Floor, Castle House,
75–76 Wells Street, London W1T 3QH

1 3 5 7 9 10 8 6 4 2

Designed and typeset by Jerry Goldie

Printed and bound in Malaysia by Imago

British Library Cataloguing-in-Publication data available

ISBN: 978-1-905857-18-0

www.watkinspublishing.com

CONTENTS

THE PREFATORY QUATRAINS

THE RETROSPECTIVE QUATRAINS

THE GOOD NEWS QUATRAINS

ACKNOWLEDGMENTS

As is always the case with books as complex as this one is to proof, edit, and research, I have a number of people to thank for their help during the parturition process: Bert Plusquin, for first taking me to the Great Treasury at Aachen [*see* quatrain 7/41] and for describing so beautifully how the Allied bombers managed to avoid destroying what is arguably the symbolic cradle of Europe; my editor, Michael Mann, for his consistent friendship and much valued advice; Shelagh Boyd, for both her friendship and her editing skills; Penny Stopa, for her ever-cheerful help with the production details – even when I inadvertently filled out one of her authors' questionnaires on the wrong book; and finally my wife, Claudia, without whose presence the whole thing wouldn't make any sense anyway.

Habent Sua Fata Libelli

—

Books Have Their Own Destiny

From Terentianus Maurus's *De Litteris Syllabis Et Metris Horatii* (Ed: Georgius Galbiatus), Milan, Uldericus Scinzenzeler, 4 February 1497

For my late sister-in-law,
Maria 'Titi' del Carmen Fautsch de Villarreal

INTRODUCTION

Whenever I've given radio interviews or appeared on documentaries or news broadcasts in the course of writing about Nostradamus, one question has always thrust itself inexorably to the fore. Was Nostradamus always doom and gloom, or did he ever get around to predicting any good news? Fascinated by this idea, I returned to the complete Nostradamian *Centuries* and scoured them for any faint inklings of hope. To my immense surprise, I discovered that Nostradamus was a great deal more positive than people give him credit for, and that there was at the very least a good book's worth of *Good News* quatrains to be teased out from amongst the horrors and intimations of Armageddon and the End Of Days that recidivist Jonahs and vainglorious commentators have always been so keen to associate with his work.

Good news is, by its very nature, subjective – somebody's good news is, after all, frequently only somebody else's worst nightmare. I have tried to get around this inconvenient fact by choosing only quatrains that appear to offer, for the most part at least, generalised good news. But this is not always, of course, possible. My second line of defence, therefore, is to choose quatrains that suggest that the 'goodies' (or at the very least the 'ethically responsible') will be the eventual winners. I have taken this line because it was Nostradamus's most fundamental belief that if the world could only see into the future, it would wish to alter it benevolently. His prophecies may be construed, therefore, as in part an attempt to communicate across the intervening ages with the world to come, and in further part to cause that world to change itself *before it is too late* to the advantage of all humanity. As a direct consequence it became inevitable that *Nostradamus: The Good News* would isolate only those prophecies which suggested such a possibility of creative change, allowing the prophecies, and Nostradamus himself, to be shown, for the first time ever, in an entirely fresh and forward-looking light. These are the prophecies that did – and indeed *could* – alter the world for the better.

I should perhaps come clean now and say that people anticipating a simple rehash of previous famous predictions are going to be seriously disappointed, for I have approached each quatrain with entirely fresh eyes, and translated it without any recourse to either earlier translations or erstwhile set-in-stone interpretations. To achieve this end I have occasionally used a technique of my own invention which I call 'euphonic translation'. This technique takes into account the crucial importance, whilst translating Nostradamus, of bearing in mind the actual *sound* of the line (alongside its more literal, conventional interpretation, needless to say), together with the often hidden meanings potentially contained within those sounds. The fact that many commentators have never cottoned on to this possibility (despite French being the euphonic language that it is!) and have therefore restricted themselves slavishly to the written and often misprinted text – they are thinking purely linearly, in other words – often limits access to possible meanings which should, and in my opinion, do, inform the whole. The proof, of course, is in the pudding.

In some cases, where either or all possible meanings (the literal, the metaphorical, and the codified) may need to be taken into account, I have put the second, subsidiary (or non-linear) meaning in brackets. A good example occurs in 10/89 – 1789 [The French Revolution] – it comes in line 3, with the word *Laqueduict*. The word may be taken literally, as a misprinting for *L'Aqueduct* (an aqueduct), or it may be taken euphonically as *Là qu'eux dit* (literally, 'that which was said, by them, there'). In my view Nostradamus often signals such bilateral readings by the purposeful misspelling of an obvious word, or its inclusion in a place where its objective reading makes no sense whatsoever (whereas its euphonic reading does). He can then rely on the tunnel vision common to most scholars – i.e. that there must be a literal answer to everything, or the world cannot possibly make sense – to protect his hidden meanings. I, on the other hand, am neither a scholar, and nor do I feel that the world necessarily needs to make sense (I believe in God – *He* makes sense) – I therefore hold no truck whatsoever with such unnecessary and crippling limitations. As a (hopefully enlightened) commentator I am simply out to get as close to Nostradamus's core meaning as possible, and if that involves a few unforced errors, well then, so be it – I beg the forgiveness of my readers.

Another thing I entirely fail to understand is why commentators pay such scant attention to Nostradamus's own index numbers. I am speaking of the first and second numbers, separated by a slash, which identify each quatrain – the first number refers quite simply to which one of the series of ten (or possibly twelve) groups of a hundred verses it adheres to, whereas the second number, after the slash, would appear to refer to a specific year within a particular lineal, but non-specific (until teased out) century. Is it somehow written in stone that these numbers cannot possibly be right? If so, I've never discovered the source. Surely Nostradamus would only have needed to conceal dates that occurred within the span of his own lifetime, if the reason for that concealment was to stifle potentially painful inquiries by the Inquisition – the rest, by default, wouldn't matter! Usually, but not always, I can then go on to match the index date to circumstances in a matching past – or, more speculatively, a future – year, and which find themselves reflected more than once (and by preference at least three times) within the quatrain. This done, I then feel able to date the quatrain, and engage on my commentary. It is only when this technique fails, that I ascribe a more tentative index date to the quatrain, based on the historical event or events to which the quatrain would seem to be pointing.

This has led me to a series of extraordinary discoveries which would not have been possible if I had not chosen to take this somewhat unconventional course. Without recourse to Nostradamus's own index numbers, for instance, I would never have discovered 7/3 – 1803 [Toussaint L'Ouverture & Haïtian Independence], or 8/53 – 1553 [John Dudley & Lady Jane Grey], not to mention 8/69 – 1669 [Antonio Stradivari] or 1/95 – 1695 [Johann Sebastian Bach]. 10/4 – 1704 [The Battle Of Blenheim] would have made no sense whatsoever, and I might have assumed that 1/76 – 1776

[The Declaration Of Independence] referred simply to Napoleon Bonaparte, as generations of commentators have chosen to believe before me. I challenge anyone, however, to read my radically new interpretations of the text and not to, at the very least, admit to a tentative reconsideration of their former position.

I should perhaps say now that I have checked my French texts meticulously against all the remaining original printings (i.e. the Bonhomme 'Lyons', the 'Utrecht' Du Rosne 'Lyons', the Du Rosne 'Lyons' itself, and the Benoist Rigaud 'Lyons') and have indicated, in brackets, where there are disparities between the different editions that might afford a potentially different reading. I have also, as mentioned in my previous book, *Nostradamus: The Complete Prophecies For The Future* (Watkins 2006), taken particular care in my renditions of the classical references and mythologies in Nostradamus's writings, for Nostradamus would, like any educated man in sixteenth-century France, have had a vast body of classical learning at his fingertips, and would have considered its use, and his readers' understanding of classical myth, as a *sine qua non*. A similar wellhead of knowledge needs to be used when interpreting the quatrains today, and negates any half-baked ideas that Nostradamus wrote in a secret, or Green Language, accessible only to privileged initiates, or to those versed in the secret lore of the Akashic Chronicle. He was, quite simply, extremely well read and well educated.

The key to Nostradamus, in my opinion, lies in the actual process of translation – the act of translating opens the commentator's mind to what Nostradamus, through the centuries (both literally and metaphorically) is trying to tell him. The commentator must therefore approach each of the quatrains with an open mind, and with the capacity to be surprised in a serendipitous manner. I trust that, when you read the commentaries which follow, you will feel that I have achieved this.

BIOGRAPHICAL NOTE

The idea that any historian is 'right', or is creating more than yet another more believable and interesting myth to overlay and influence an already existing myth, is fundamentally absurd. Few people can even describe the day that has just passed accurately – let alone decades, if not centuries, before their own time. No, what they are giving is an opinion, and a vastly subjective one at that, dependent on the often sparse material that has been left, frequently as a result of random historical happenstance, and to which they inevitably ascribe – because they have a vested interest in so doing – far too much significance. The winners in history customarily hide what is inconvenient to them, or manipulate the truth to suit the scale of their ambitions, and the losers bleat, or are written out of history altogether (Mithraism being but one obvious example) – that is, after all, human nature. When losers do out-survive those they feel have done them (or their cabal) wrong, as often as not they try to rewrite history the better to reinforce their feelings of outrage and despair – that too is human nature. All history is therefore fiction disguised as fact, but actually representing the historians' best shot at an almost-truth. It is for exactly this reason that apocryphal stories, hearsay, and scandal are potentially just as historically relevant as (purported) dry facts, government documents (a likely story), and contemporary commentaries (untarnished, of course, by even the merest hint of vainglory!).

Wars have been fought over lesser issues than the details of Nostradamus's alleged biography. So-called scholars have been declaring that only they know the true story from as far back as the late sixteenth century, and their descendants still continue to do so today (and with equal impunity). So little is actually known about Nostradamus's life, however, that some of the more apocryphal stories, often stemming from a century or so after his death, become important pointers in themselves – not so much to the 'real life' (as if anyone is capable of teasing that out from the mass of obfuscation, forgery and hearsay that underlies much Nostradamus scholarship) as to the life he ought to have led, given the reality of his influence. Anyway, here is a short biographical note that does not purport to be the exact truth (what can?) so much as to coalesce both given, disputed, and established facts into some sort of sensible (if inevitably fallible) order.

Nostradamus was both a Catholic and a Jew. If that sounds like a paradox, it wasn't perceived as such in a sixteenth-century France dedicated to both God, in the form of the Inquisition, and mammon, in the form of the pillaging of others' property for reasons of ecclesiastical expediency.

For thirty years, under the reign of Good King René, the Jews of Provence had been accorded the free practice of their religion, but all that ended with René's death in 1480, a date which unfortunately coincided with the inception of the Spanish Inquisition. By the time of Nostradamus's birth, in 1503, most prominent Jews had prudently converted to a pragmatic form of Catholicism, thanks to the edicts of, respectively, Charles VIII in 1488, and Louis XII in 1501. This didn't prevent the French Crown from occasionally plundering their possessions, but it did offer them a measure of protection in a country suddenly rife with religious intolerance and paranoia. So the infant Michel de Nostredame found himself both uncircumcised (the penalty for which, under Levitical Law, is ostracism from the congregation of Israel), and baptised according to the Christian Rite, whilst retaining, in the form of his maternal great-grandfather, Jean de Saint-Rémy, an intimate access to the Jewish chain of tradition known as the *Schalscheleth Hakabbālah*, which was to stand him in very good stead in his later incarnation as a diviner and scryer.

As a result of this upbringing, Nostradamus almost certainly dabbled in magic, and very certainly in mysticism and the Kabbalah, which encapsulated the Jewish search for new wisdom in a creative synthesis between the mythologies of ancient Egypt, ancient Greece, Assyrian astrology, Babylonian magic, Arabian divination and Platonic philosophy. The secretive and mystical nature of the Kabbalah provided a much-needed escape from the grim realities of Jewish life in an Inquisitorial Europe, and a much-needed panacea in the face of the forcible conversions that followed René's death. By pure chance, Nostradamus's native town of St-Rémy was the perfect place to study the Kabbalah, as Provence was generally acknowledged as home to the earliest Kabbalistic community in France. Paradoxically, perhaps, Nostradamus, as well as being a Kabbalist, an alchemist, and a Talmudist, was also a fervent adherent to Catholic doctrine throughout his life, and would certainly not have been accepted at Avignon University (not then a part of France) had he not been sincere in these assertions, and in his excoriations of the near ubiquitous Lutheran heresy. He later enrolled, again without problem, at the venerable University of Montpellier (founded in 1220) in order to study medicine – a wise move, as Montpellier possessed, without doubt, the greatest school of medicine of those times.

Following on from his matriculation from Montpellier* – which would have been conducted in the medieval manner of a formal, invigilated dispute between the student and the teaching staff, rather than by written examination – Nostradamus was plunged straight into the treatment of an outbreak of the plague. Encumbered by the usual paraphernalia worn by medical practitioners during such crises (leather jerkin, glasses, sponge mask, and a coat stained with many different coloured powders), Nostradamus struck out

* Some commentators insist that he was expelled from Montpellier for the alleged crime of having practised as an apothecary – a somewhat unlikely story, as there is ample evidence that he was styled as 'doctor' by both correspondents, publishers, and even kings in later life.

into entirely new territory with his invention of a purifying powder (his 'rose pill'), which, we are led to believe, inspired an entirely untypical confidence in his patients. As a direct consequence of this experience, Nostradamus became something of an authority on the plague, a talent that was sorely tested when plague struck, once again, during his tenure as a doctor at Agen, killing his young wife and their two children. As a result, Nostradamus not only suffered from the usual criticism of 'Physician, heal thyself', but was also sued by the distraught family of his wife for the return of her dowry.

Traumatised by his loss, Nostradamus took to the road, and travelled through many parts of France, Italy and Sicily, before finally settling in Salon de Provence. There, at the age of forty-four, he met a widow, Anne Ponsarde Gemelle, whom he married on the 11th November 1547. They moved into a house on the rue Ferreiraux (now known as rue Nostradamus), and Nostradamus, in considerable demand by this time, not least for his sovereign remedies, continued his travels. It was during this period that, thanks to his meetings with apothecaries, physicians and magicians, he first began to suspect that he had the gift of prophecy and second sight. He was not the only one, of course. Under the reign of the thirteen Valois kings, it was estimated that there were upwards of 30,000 astrologers, sorcerers, alchemists and prophets practising in Paris alone, and it is to Nostradamus's credit, and to that of his art, that he rose, inexorably, to the top of a very crowded tree.

Three years after the publication of his *Traité Des Fardemens* in 1552 (an *à la mode* treatise on unguents, jams and preserves of all kinds), Nostradamus followed up – rather tentatively, it must be said – with the first edition of his famous *Les Prophéties* (1555), fearing, according to his pupil, Jean Aymes de Chavigny, both castigation and mockery. The 353 quatrains, to just about everybody's surprise, including that of Nostradamus, were a sensation. Summoned to Paris by Henri II's queen, Catherine de Medici, barely a year after publication, Nostradamus returned to Salon a rich man, having discovered, the hard way, that private practice (the casting of personal horoscopes and the alleviation of courtiers' ailments) was considerably more remunerative, and a good deal less precarious, than celebrity stargazing.

Nostradamus continued to advise Catherine, though, not least because she protected him, in some measure, from falling foul of the religious authorities for blasphemy, while her regal favour afforded him a much-appreciated kudos and the promise of a steady income. The summit of his celebrity career came during a royal visit to Salon itself, in 1564, by the boy king, Charles IX (who would later, at his dominant mother's instigation, approve the St Bartholomew's Day Massacre). Catherine invited Nostradamus and his family to a private visit at the royal apartments, and then to a further consultation, where she asked him to cast the horoscope of her youngest son, the Duke of Anjou. Nostradamus was more interested in the young Henri de Navarre [*see* 4/93 – 1593: Good King Henry Of Navarre], however, and even investigated the ten-year-old child while he was sleeping, predicting that he would eventually inherit all of France.

Nostradamus was well paid for his troubles, which must have provided considerable comfort during his two declining years, for, assailed by gout, arthritis and a heart condition that even his own sovereign remedies failed to alleviate, he finally succumbed on the 2nd July 1566, in exactly the fashion he had predicted for himself.

THE PREFATORY QUATRAINS

✦

In which Nostradamus attempts to explain both his motivations and his techniques in the form of five key quatrains, which were intended to act as a direct preface to the *Centuries*, explaining and sharing the source of his visions to a potential future audience.

NOSTRADAMUS EXPLAINS HIS TECHNIQUE

Etant assis de nuit secret étude,

Seul repose (repousé) sus la selle d'aerain,

Flambe exigue sortant de solitude,

Fait proferer (prosperer) qui n'est à croire vain.

Finally seated, at night, in secret study

At rest and alone over the bronze stool

A slender flame emerges from the wilderness

Unbelievable deeds are uttered from the wasteland.

What is interesting about this quatrain is the position Nostradamus accords himself when divining – 'over' the bronze stool or tripod. This correlates with what we have heard about his divining techniques, namely that after preparing himself with spiritual exercises and copious amounts of hallucination-enhancing nutmeg, he would stoop over a bowl of ink-stained water, a cloth spread about his head to avoid residual light, and then, by means of meditation, enter a trance-like state, becoming possessed by what he called the 'spirits of the void' (it is instructive to note here that in the Old French, *solitude*, in line 3, and *vain*, in line 4, mean a wasteland, a waste, a wilderness, or a void, and not 'solitude' or 'vain', as many translators have wrongly supposed).

Nostradamus probably adapted his technique from that expounded by the fourth-century Syrian neo-Platonist philosopher and student of Porphyry, Iamblicus Chalcidensis, in his treatise, the *Theurgia*, or *De Mysteriis Aegyptiorum*, which was reprinted in Lyons in 1547. Iamblicus speaks of the divining methods used by the Persian Zoroastrian priests, or Magi, in an effort to interpret and influence the battle between darkness and light (*Aša*/the truth and *Druj*/the lie). This eternal struggle would also have been much on Nostradamus's mind as he attempted to see into the wastes, and to influence future behaviour for the eventual good of humanity.

SUMMARY

Nostradamus describes how he approaches the act of scrying/divining.

NOSTRADAMUS ENTERS INTO A TRANCE

La verge en maï (main) mise au milieu de branches
De l'onde il mouille et le limbe et le pied:
Un peur et voix fremissent par les manches,
Splendeur divine. Le Divin prés s'assied.

The hawthorn rod is placed at the centre of
the tripod

He wets both his limbs and his feet with
the wavelets

Fear and a trembling voice. He is in its power.

Divine splendour. God is near. He sits.

It is at least arguable that Nostradamus believed in the 'Manifestation Of God' as depicted in Bahá'í Zoroastrianism, in which certain key prophets were called upon to gradually reveal the Word of God to a steadily maturing and therefore progressively more amenable world. To that extent Nostradamus no doubt imagined that he had been genuinely touched by God when he first became aware of his powers during his wanderings following the death of his first wife and two children in the plague – and therefore his reference to being in the actual presence of God should not be taken as *lèse majesté*, but rather as a recognition of his conviction that his powers were God, rather than Devil, driven.

When taken with 1/1 – 1555 [Nostradamus Explains His Technique], therefore, what we are given is a pretty clear picture of the sort of ritual Nostradamus went through before essaying a connection with what he called the 'void' or 'wasteland'. The mention of the hawthorn rod (*la verge en maï*) is of particular interest here, as the Romans considered hawthorn a charm against sorcery and lightning, and were wont to place leaves from its branches across the cots of newly born children (hawthorn being sacred to the Roman goddess Maia Maiestas). There is also a connection between the word *maï*, the French word *magi* (magic) and the Magi, suggested in the previous quatrain, as all the words arguably come from the same root, namely the Latin *maius/Magius*, which corresponds to the Sanskrit word *mah*, meaning to 'grow'. Hawthorn, in addition, is often used for dowsing, as it responds well to water (being traditionally connected to holy wells), and this direction-seeking aspect is doubtless why Nostradamus places the stick at the exact centre of the water-filled tripod.

Summary

Nostradamus continues with the explanation of his scrying techniques, and attempts to prove that they are God, and not Devil, driven – in an effort, no doubt, to ward off the attentions of the Inquisition, and to prove to nay-sayers that they were meant benevolently.

ALCHEMY & THE
SACRED MARRIAGE

3 / 2

Le divin verbe donrra à la substance,

Comprins cie, terre, or occult au faict mystique

Corps, ame, esprit ayant toute puissance

Tant sous ses pieds, comme au siege celique.

The word of God will give to the substance –

Which comprises heaven, earth, and the
alchemist's golden secret –

A body, soul, and spirit of all-consuming power

On Earth and in Hell (beneath its feet),
just as in Heaven's seat.

Gold was the alchemical sun (and therefore a fundamentally male entity, symbolic of the Light of God), and the transmutation of base metals (the female seed) into gold was one of the three great goals of the alchemists, alongside the discovery of the universal solvent and the elixir of life. Alchemy itself was known as the *Ars Magna*, or secret science, from the Arabic word *al kímía* (the secret art), so it is hardly surprising that the English word 'chemistry' stems from the very same root. The four principle alchemical elements were linked to the four primary colours in the following combinations: Fire/Red (hot and dry), Air/Yellow (hot and wet), Water/Green (cold and wet) and Earth/Blue (cold and dry), representing, between them, Nature (the primaries) and the Spirit (white, black and orange, often in the form of sandalwood). Through a tacit combination of all or some of these, a divine or sacred marriage (the *Conjunctio* – or the material made spirit) might conceivably be consummated, equivalent, in one sense, to the marriage of the quaternary (Fire, Earth, Air and Water) and the ternary (Sulphur, Salt and Mercury).

Nostradamus is therefore describing the Great Void [*see* 1/1 and 1/2 – 1555: Nostradamus Explains His Technique and Nostradamus Enters Into A Trance], which is an alchemical euphemism for the fundamental 'ground of the being', in the sense that it is both dynamic and stable at the same time, and finds itself contained of memory, in the form of what C G Jung called the 'Collective Unconscious' – in that sense the void could be said to correspond to a blank page, or to a blank slate awaiting mystic revelation. Nostradamus makes it very clear in these three great quatrains that when he enters one of his scrying trances, he feels that he is connecting with this void or wasteland, and that it is inhabiting him (and he, it) in the form of an Hermetic Identity. That what may seem divine revelation is in fact a chemical/mystical occurrence triggered through the placing of the tree of knowledge (in the symbolical form of a hawthorn branch) into the exact centre of the divine elixir, or water of life (in the symbolical form of the darkened water bowl). It is this sacred marriage of Spirit and Materia which was to both form and contain the basis of his divinatory powers.

Summary

Nostradamus moves on to the mystical and spiritual connotations of the art of scrying, and explains some of the minutiae of Hermetic Identity. In so doing, he also reveals the sources of his divinatory power.

NOSTRADAMUS CRACKS A JOKE

Legis Cantio Contra Ineptos Criticos

Quos legent hosce versus maturè censunto,
Profanum vulgus, et inscium ne attrestato
Omnesq: Astrologi Blenni, Barbari procul sunto,
Qui alter facit, is ritè, sacer esto.

Herewith An Incantatory Edict Against Inept Critics

Pay attention, readers of these verses

And may the profane and ignorant rabble not feel giddy

Idiot astrologers and barbarians too may stay away

And those who won't, go stuff yourselves.

Nostradamus's only Latin prophecy is a gently amusing skit on a quintain/cinquain (a five-line verse) he originally discovered in Petrus Crinitus's *Comentarii De Honesta Disciplina* (1504), and which runs as follows:

> Legis cautio contra Ineptos criticos:
> Quoi legent hosce libros mature censunto.
> Profanum vulgus et inscium ne attrectato:
> Omnesque legulei, blenni, barbari procul sunto.
> Qui aliter faxit, is rite sacer esto.

Curious, no? And why the changes? I think Nostradamus simply liked what he saw and decided to annexe it, all the while adding a few nugatory wrinkles of his own. The first line resembles the 'hear ye, hear ye' shout of the town crier, and the remaining four lines read like a skit on a papal bull, or, even more to the point, a doctor's prescription. So Nostradamus is 'prescribing' for his readers, and telling them to watch out for mountebanks, quacks and charlatans, and to take whatever such impertinent critics say with the proverbial pinch of salt. All in all, it's rather comforting to feel that Nostradamus had a sense of humour, which he had also showed to good effect four years earlier, in 1553, when asked to provide a Latin inscription for a new water fountain in Salon. He came up with the following: 'If human ingenuity had been capable of providing Salon's citizens with a never-ending supply of wine, the Senate and Magistrates of Salon would scarcely have needed, at significant cost, and during the consulships of Paul Antoine and

Palamède Marc, to erect this commonplace water fountain which you now find before you.'

Summary

Nostradamus makes fun of his future critics, and warns his readers to take what such people say with an anticipatory pinch of salt.

NOSTRADAMUS DEFENDS HIS CORNER

1557

9/81

Le Roi rusé entendra ses embusches

De trois quartiers ennemis assaillir

Un nombre estranges larmes de coqueluches

Viendra Lemprin du traducteur faillir.

The cunning king is a master of ambush

His enemies threaten him on three sides

A strange number, and the tears of monks

The translator's brilliance will fail him.

This quatrain is a prime example of the necessity of what I have chosen, in my introduction, to call 'euphonic translation' – i.e. translation directly from the sound rather than from what appears to be written (and which might otherwise make no sense). It has long been understood that all codified material must be approached both literally and laterally, and a particularly good example of that necessity occurs in the first line of this quatrain, which may be read literally as 'The cunning king is a master of ambush', or laterally as 'The artful king will hearken to his mouthpiece' – in the lateral context I have taken *embusches* to suggest *embouchure*, a reading further reinforced by the listening aspect of *entendra*, which can mean both 'listening', 'understanding' and 'agreeing', depending on context. Continuing with this lateral approach – which Nostradamus himself appears to be advocating thanks to his jibe at the shortcomings of his translators, in line 4 – we achieve an alternative translation, as follows:

> The artful king will hearken to his mouthpiece
> The enemy will attack from two or three
> different directions
> A curious number of hooded tears
> He will arrive, and his calumniator's borrowing
> will fail.

So we are left with an intelligent, even Confucian king, who is wise enough to listen to advice and who, despite being assailed from a number of different sides by his enemies, manages to see through the 'crocodile tears' of those closest to him and end up by outwitting all those who wish to damage him by their lies. Sound familiar? Yes, it's touchy old Nostradamus justifying himself, yet again, in the face of expected future criticism. Which all goes to show that he really did believe that his work would have importance for future generations, and wished to forestall the nay-sayers before they gained an incontrovertible foothold.

Summary

Nostradamus disguises himself and his quatrain beneath more than the usual number of obfuscatory layers – an amusing example of shutting the stable door considerably before the horse has actually bolted. Convinced of the creative value of his quatrains, he does not wish their transformatory power to be diluted.

THE
RETROSPECTIVE
QUATRAINS

✦

In which Nostradamus attempts to influence
mankind's future behaviour by reference to
situations and events that occurred in the past
and which he feels may reoccur, in a similar
pattern, at some time in the future. By using the
past as a template, he hopes to influence future
behaviour patterns in a benevolent and
constructive way.

THE SECOND COMING
OF JESUS CHRIST

8–2 BC ONWARDS

8 / 27

La voye auxelle l'une sur l'autre fornix
Du muy deser hor mis brave et genest,
L'escript d'empereur le fenix
Veu en celuy ce qu'à nul autre n'est.

The way in which one arches on top of the other

The brave young one is placed in the great desert
outside

The laws of the emperor mean nothing to him

He wishes on one for that which no other
can have.

Brothels were known as *fornixes* (arches) in ancient Rome, because prostitutes were apparently in the habit of gathering under the arches of the bridges, aqueducts and walkways near the River Tiber in order the better to conduct their business – not uncoincidentally, perhaps, the vaginal fornix is the arched vault created by the protrusion of the cervix into the vagina. Much of the rest of the quatrain needs to be translated euphonically (*see* Introduction), or it makes no sense whatsoever. *Muy*, for instance, becomes the Spanish for 'great' rather than the locational Le Muy in Provence – *genest* becomes *jeunesse* (youth), as well as implying a jennet (a small Spanish horse or donkey) – and *le fenix*, as well as suggesting a phoenix (in the sense of something that rises from the ashes of a previous incarnation) also gives us *le fait nix*, meaning 'doesn't affect him' or 'means nothing to him'. Now with all these clues in place, namely the interior of the vagina (a virgin birth?), the desert (the forty days in the wilderness – Mark 1: 9–13), the young man (Jesus), the donkey (the entry into Bethlehem), the emperor (Augustus), and the unique singularity implied within the last line, it seems to me that we are being given the story of Christ.

But why is Nostradamus hiding his meaning in this way? And why does he use both euphemism and dysphemism (in the sense of *fornix*)? Could he be describing the Second Coming of Christ, this time to be born of a prostitute (the Great Whore?). That would certainly explain Nostradamus's caution in making his meaning clear, and also the presence of the phoenix in line 3. In addition, it appears next to impossible to ascribe a clear date to Nostradamus's quatrain.

In my view this is because Nostradamus would not have wished to be seen (particularly by the Inquisition) to have been prejudging or anticipating what should, and could, only be within God's own remit. All the clues are there, however, for in the Esoteric tradition there is both a Christ Without and a Christ Within, and Nostradamus's 'arch' symbolism in the first line describes this intertwining perfectly – this would also explain his statement that 'the laws of the emperor mean nothing to him', for the Second Advent of Christ presupposes a judgment that is 'beyond the human', echoing the sense of the following words, which are to be found within the Nicene Creed: 'And he shall come again, with glory, to judge both the quick and the dead: Whose Kingdom will have no end:' (from The Book of Common Prayer)

Summary

Nostradamus looks forward to the Second Coming of Christ, using terms that would be more understandable to adherents of the Esoteric Christian tradition of the early Essenes and later (pre- and post-Nostradamian) Rosicrucians, rather than to adherents of the modernist Christian movement. The quatrain is decidedly upbeat, however, and appears to suggest that Christ's Second Coming will, indeed, be a matter of extreme, and unique, 'good news'.

NOSTRADAMUS LAUDS PROGRESSIVE CHANGE

466/1566

5/66

Soubs les antiques edifices vestaulx,

Non esloignez d'aqueduct ruyné:

De Sol et Lune sont les luisans metaulx,

Ardante lampe Traian d'or buriné.

Beneath the ancient vestal structures

Not far removed from the ruined aqueduct

The shining metals of Sol and Luna

Trajan's fiery lamp engraved with gold.

Traian, as well as being a prominent Hungarian name (for reasons which I will explain later), is also the name of the second of the five 'good' Roman emperors, Marcus Ulpius Nerva Traianus (a.k.a. Trajan) – indeed the Senate even went so far as to confer on Trajan the title of *Optimus*, meaning 'the best', in honour of his fair-mindedness. Fond of his wine – and even fonder of the occasional handsome youth – Trajan was nevertheless most notable from his military successes, amongst which his campaign against the Dacians (modern Romania, Moldova, incorporating parts of Bulgaria, Hungary and the Ukraine) stands supreme. During this campaign, which lasted between 101 and 106 AD, Trajan, using a design by the famous Greek architect Appolodorus of Damascus, built a massive bridge ('the ruined aqueduct') over the Danube. The bridge spanned all 800 metres of the river, extending onto both banks for a further 170 metres on each side. It was 15 metres wide, and its base was 19 metres above the water, with two Castri (towers) at either end. Despite being destroyed by the Emperor Aurelian following Rome's eventual withdrawal from Dacian territory, in Nostradamus's time at least twenty pillars of the bridge were still clearly visible to the naked eye (down to about two, today, thanks to time, flood erosion, and wanton destruction).

The mention of *Sol*, *Luna*, and the *vestal* virgins, also reinforces the Roman connection, as Sol Invictus (or Oriens) was the principle divinity of the Roman pantheon (post Trajan, it has to be said), and accorded with sunlight and the east in terms of symbolical value (and with Helios, in the Greek pantheon, from whence it sprung). Sol and Luna were also the names given by the ancient alchemists to gold and silver, with gold being the fundamental aim of all alchemical endeavour, both in terms of the transmutation of metals, and the formation of the universal solvent/elixir of life. 'Trajan's fiery lamp' also accords with the mention of the six vestal virgins, whose duty it was to keep Vesta's lamp perpetually burning (alongside, and premised upon, the retaining of their chastity). Vesta (known by the Greeks as Hestia) was the Roman goddess of the home and hearth, and she, through her acolytes, was responsible for the maintenance and occasional reconstitution of the sacred fire that Aeneas brought with him from Troy, and upon which Rome's foundation was also premised.

The obvious implication, therefore, through a juxtaposition of the 'ruined aqueduct' and the 'fiery lamp' of Trajan (Traian/*Troyen*/Trojan), is that mighty empires do eventually crumble away into dust, and that sacred fires do indeed burn out, and that these eventualities hold long-term ramifications for the vainglorious. Indeed the penalty for a vestal virgin for losing her chastity and thus tainting the Sacred Fire, was living entombment in the Campus Sceleratus (near the Colline gate, just outside ancient Rome) – a symbolical living death, in other words. The year 466 (*see* index date), did indeed see the Huns invading Dacia, but being temporarily repelled by the Byzantine Emperor, Leo I (the final, blazing precursor to the utter dissolution of the Western Roman Empire ten years later), whilst the year 1566 saw Nostradamus's own, self-predicted, death.

Summary

Using both the Roman and Trojan empires as examples, Nostradamus cautions potentates (and reassures the meek) that great empires are always finite, and that, as with alchemy and human life, history defines itself by a continuous process of melding, transmogrification, and necessary reconstitution.

THE *BLANCHE NEF* (WHITE SHIP)

8 / 5

Apparoistra temple luisant orné,

La lampe et cierge à Borne et Breteuil.

Pour la lucerne le canton destorné,

Quand on verra le grand coq au cercueil.

A church will be built, shining and much adorned

The lamp and the candle at Borne and Breteuil

The canton turns aside because of La Lucerne

When the great cock is finally in his coffin.

Given that Breteuil is in Normandy, it seems strange that previous commentators haven't bothered to look in Normandy for a La Lucerne, but have simply chosen to make the assumption that Nostradamus is, by default, talking of Switzerland. In the event the twelfth-century abbey of La Lucerne is situated in the bay of Mont St Michel, on the exact same latitude as Breteuil, and with the department of the Orne (yes Orne, not Borne) directly in between – all, of course, are in Normandy. Extraordinarily, just as Nostradamus predicted, the abbey is in the process of being rebuilt – according to the abbey website, it has been 'rising from its ruins since 1959', and major works were also carried out in the period 1989–99.

Every year, on the night of the 24th to the 25th November, the great abbey bell tolls softly all night long in mourning for young Prince William the Aethling, son of Henry I of England, and grandson of William the Conqueror, and also of his tutor, Othoërne, father of the founder of La Lucerne, Hasculfe de Subligny, both of whom drowned as a result of the sinking of the *Blanche Nef*, at Barfleur, in 1120. The Captain of the *Blanche Nef*, Thomas Fitz Stephen, actually survived the sinking, but when he saw that William – who died trying to save his sister – together with his illegitimate brother, Richard, and his natural born half-sister, Princess Matilda, had all perished, he threw himself back into the sea to share their fate and that of the 140 knights and 18 noblewomen who accompanied them. It is said that after King Henry ('the great cock') heard of the disaster, he never smiled again.

Nostradamus harks back to a tragedy that changed the map of medieval Europe and arguably even prepared the way for the Protestant Reformation, thanks to Henry VIII's fears (triggered by the succession crisis that resulted from the wreck), that England would never again accept to be governed by a female heir. The Protestant Reformation, however, had the perverse good effect of actually ensuring the possibility of a female succession, in the form of Queen Elizabeth I.

THE BRITISH INVASION OF FRANCE

Au mois troisième se levant le Soleil,
Sanglier, Liepard, aux champs Mars pour combatre:
Liepard laisse au Ciel extend son oeil,
Un Aigle autour du Soleil voit s'esbatre.

In the third month, at the rising of the sun

The wild boar and the leopard meet on the battlefield

The leashed leopard raises his eye to heaven

And sees an eagle beating around the sun.

In medieval France the leopard traditionally represented the English, thanks to the French Heralds' description of the English device as a *lion leopardé*. Bertrand du Guesclin, Constable of France from 1370–80 (his heart is kept at the basilica of Saint-Sauveur at Dinan) famously proclaimed that '*les hommes devoyent bien honorer la noble Fleur-de-lis, plus qu'ils ne faisaient le félon Liépard*' ('men should rather honour the noble Fleur-de-lis, than the treacherous leopard'). Continuing with the heraldic note, however, we also find the leopard representing brave and generous warriors who have acquitted themselves honourably in some bold enterprise. The 'wild boar', as well as being an emblem of warlike fury and merciless brutality, also doubled as the cognisance of Richard III, and of Guillaume, Conte de la Marck (the 'wild boar of the Ardennes'), as well as of the present author's de Reading ancestors (Simon de Reading having been hung, drawn and quartered alongside his friend, Hugh Despenser, in 1326, for the alleged crime of having insulted the queen and snatching the lands of Roger Mortimer's follower, John Wyard).

The eagle, on the other hand, as well as being the emblem of the French Empire, is also the emblem of St John the Evangelist, for he, like the eagle, allegedly gazed upon 'the sun of glory'. The eagle, in this context, was the only one of God's creatures considered capable of being able to stare directly into the sun's heart, for when it became old and infirm, the bird was apparently in the habit of launching itself, like an arrow, straight towards the golden orb, which would then melt away the calcified deposits of old age and renew its youth (Psalm 103: 5). St John was therefore reckoned to have inherited the eagle's aegis because he, in his Gospels, was judged to have seen most clearly into the divinity of Christ 'as the light'.

So what are we left with? Warfare between the French and the English, capture, and then resurrection – and all contained within an index date of 23. This would suggest a retrospective quatrain, therefore, dealing with the invasion of France, via Calais, by the British in 1523, under Charles Brandon, 1st Duke of Suffolk, during the Four Years War (an invasion that had been secretly planned, via the Treaty of Bruges, to occur before March 1523 – the 'third month'). This belated invasion was at first wildly successful, and Suffolk drove his military wedge as far as the Somme, devastating the French countryside, and only stopping his campaign fifty miles short of Paris. Without the promised support from the Holy Roman Emperor, Charles V, however, Suffolk decided against a siege of Paris, and eventually withdrew his forces back to Calais.

Summary

A really rather cheery quatrain, which appears to be pointing up England's long-standing perfidy against France, and suggesting, via the symbol of the imperial eagle, that France will eventually gain the upper hand (possibly thanks to divine intervention in the likes of a somewhat recalcitrant Holy Roman Emperor).

FOUNDATION OF THE LEAGUE OF GOTHA

27 FEBRUARY 1526

3/26

Des rois et princes dresseront simulacres,

Augures, cruez eslués aruspices:

Corne, victime d'orée, et d'azur, d'acre:

Interpretés seront les extispices.

Kings and princes will set up false images of God

Augurs and haruspices will rise with the flood

Horn, a golden sacrifice, azure, pungency

The entrails will be read.

I shall take the liberty here of quoting directly from my book, *The Watkins Dictionary Of Dreams* (Watkins 2007) for reasons which, I hope, will become immediately apparent:

Augury: Augury is the art of divination, which consists in predicting what is going to happen in the future. The augurs of ancient Rome were soothsayers belonging to a priestly college who interpreted the words of the gods as they were passed down to human beings, either through the movement of birds (ornithomancy or avis-spicere) or through the taking of other auspices such as thunder and lightning, the movement of animals, the manner of feeding of chickens, or the content of dreams. Haruspices (a caste which originated in the Etruscan Disciplina and were later hijacked by the Romans), foretold the future through the observation of the entrails of sacrificial victims, as described in Cicero's *De Divinatione*.

Horns: In Greek mythology, the horn-gate was one of the two dream gates – the other was made of ivory. The horn-gate dreams were likely to come true, while those that issued from the ivory gate were deceptive in some way – this idea stemmed from puns on the Greek words for horn and ivory, namely *krano* and *elephas*, which suggested verbs meaning 'to bring to an issue' or

'to cheat', respectively. 'Two gates for ghostly
dreams there are: one gateway of honest horn,
and one of ivory. Issuing by the ivory gates are
dreams of glimmering illusion, fantasies, but
those that come through solid polished horn
may be borne out, if mortals only know them.'
(From Homer's *The Odyssey*, Book xix, ninth
century BC)

I believe, therefore, that this is a retrospective quatrain,
referring to the year 1526 (*see* index date of 26), which saw
the foundation of the League of Gotha, a group of
Protestant German princes led by John Frederick, elector of
Saxony, together with Philip, landgrave of Hesse. The League
included a whole succession of other princes, amongst which
those of Mansfeld, Brandenburg-Ansbach, Mecklenburg,
Anholt and Brunswick-Lüneberg were only the most
prominent. Nostradamus, a staunch Catholic, would no
doubt have ascribed many of the horrors of the next century
(including the Thirty Years War of 1618–48) to the founding
of this brotherhood, and might also be reasonably said to
have considered Protestantism a case of 'kings and princes
setting up false images of God'.

The year 1526 also saw the First Diet of Speyer – an
armistice, perhaps, rather than a direct annulment of the
Edict of Worms, but nevertheless immensely important to
the progress of the Reformation – which declared that 'every
State shall so live, rule, and believe as it may hope and trust
to answer before God and his imperial Majesty'. This, in
turn, led to the famous Otto von Pack fraud of 1527, in which

crooked politician von Pack duped Protestant Philip of Hesse into believing that the Catholic princes of the German-speaking nations had constructed a secret League dedicated to wiping out all the Protestants. The Reformers of Wittenberg only narrowly avoided a bloodbath after a fake copy of the document turned up – for which the naïve Philip had paid von Pack 4,000 guilders – and which was immediately proved to be a forgery.

Summary

Good news for the Catholics – whose side Nostradamus would, quite naturally, have taken – with the German Protestant princes getting egg all over their faces on account of the farcical Otto von Pack fraud. The fraud did, however, throw up interesting pointers to the way events would turn out in the run-up to the Thirty Years War, as well as providing a rare injection of humour into an otherwise mercilessly unhumourous epoch.

THE FUTURE OF THE AMERICAS

Jupiter joinct plus Venus qu'à la Lune

Apparoissant de plenitude blanche:

Venus cachée soubs la blancheur Neptune,

De Mars frappée par la granée branche.

Jupiter joined more to Venus than the Moon

It will establish itself in white fullness

Venus hidden beneath Neptune's whiteness

Struck by the seeded branch of Mars.

The planet Neptune was only discovered by the astronomers John Couch Adams, Jean Joseph Leverrier and Johann Gottfried Galle in 1846, so we know for a fact that Nostradamus is referring here to the Roman god of the sea, and not to the planet. If that is the case, then the other planetary mentions must also apply to Roman gods, namely Jupiter, the king of the gods (the alchemical tin); Venus, the goddess of love (the alchemical copper); Selene, the goddess of the full moon (the alchemical silver); Mars, the god of war (the alchemical iron); and the aforementioned Neptune, god of the sea (the alchemical bismuth – at least according to Sir Isaac Newton). So we have tin joined more to copper than to silver, followed by copper overwhelmed by bismuth, and the whole triggered by iron. Well, it could be a recipe for the transmutation of base metals into gold (copper is known to dissolve, for instance, in molten bismuth, forming a brittle and easily removable alloy, just as Nostradamus suggests in line 3) or it could be taken more metaphorically, and related to a historical event in which warfare (Mars and the use of iron) was the predominant characteristic.

Taking 33 as the index date, therefore, we find that 1533 was a signal year in the Spanish Conquest of the Americas, encompassing, as it did, Pizarro's (Mars's) execution of Atahualpa, Emperor of Peru (Jupiter); the march on Cuzco (the capital of the Inca empire, and therefore equivalent to gold); the investing of the Mayan Yucatan (also gold); and the colonisation of La Plata (meaning, quite literally, 'silver'). Is Nostradamus being critical, therefore, of the Spanish conquest of the Americas? And is he equating Spanish ambitions with the transformation of base metals into something of far greater value?

S U M M A R Y

A complex quatrain that can be read either as an optimistic take on the possibility of transmuting metals, or as a commentary on the Spanish Conquest of the Aztec, Mayan and Inca empires, a process that would eventually lead to a creative synthesis of four great cultures.

JOHN DUDLEY & LADY JANE GREY

1553

8 / 53

Dedans Boulogne voudra laver ses fautes,

Il ne pourra au temple du soleil,

Il volera faisant choses si haultes,

En hierarchie n'en fut oncq un pareil.

In Boulogne he will wish to wash away his sins

He will not be able to in the temple of the sun

He will do such high-flown things

In terms of the hierarchy, there has never been one like him.

The mention of Boulogne, in line 1, and the index date of 53, leads us inexorably to John Dudley, 1st Duke of Northumberland, and to his protégée and daughter-in-law, the short-lived, and even shorter reigning – for she was technically uncrowned – Lady Jane Grey. The mention of the 'temple of the sun' reinforces the reading, as Nostradamus would have known of the famous Inca Temple of the Sun (the Coricancha) near Cuzco, in which only true monarchs, or 'Incas', could hope to be buried.

Dudley came from a somewhat ill-starred family, as his father, Edmund Dudley, was executed following King Henry VII's death, and Dudley skipped only two reigns (those of Henry VIII and Edward VI) before succumbing to the headsman himself, under the aegis of bloody Queen Mary. In the interim, of course, he had gained a dukedom, and almost succeeded to a kingdom, in the guise of his daughter-in-law, Lady Jane Grey ('one of the finest female minds of the century') – whose head was also lopped off by the vengeful (and serially Catholic) Mary I.

Dudley had a curious relationship with 'Boulogne', too, for he both conquered it and then gave it back to the French during the course of his life, and one wonders whether this unconscious expiation wasn't behind Nostradamus's words in line 1 (for this is one of Nostradamus's rare retrospective quatrains, as it was first published in 1568, two years after Nostradamus's death, in the famous Benoist Rigaud edition of Lyons, subtitled 'Of which three hundred quatrains have never yet been printed'). Either way, it was good news for the French, as, partially thanks to the ceding of Boulogne, they were later (1558) able to take back the far greater prize of Calais (of which Queen Mary wrote: 'When I am dead and opened you shall find 'Calais' lying in my heart').

The last line beautifully sums up Dudley's career, as he was most definitely 'one of the hierarchy', and there are certainly few, if any, throughout history, who can match him in terms of nearly fulfilled ambitions – a contemporary French account speaks of him as '*de parole affable, se composant à gracieusité et doulceur, mais au dedans felon, orgueilleux, vindicatif s'il en fut jamais*' ('affable of speech, and appearing both sweet and gracious, but inside he was felonious, proud, and serially vindictive'). In Nostradamus's terms, of course, the 'good news' lies in the nominally Protestant Dudley's comeuppance at the hands of Catholic Mary, and the seeming failure of the British to be able to contrive a Protestant monarch for themselves.

Summary

The career of John Dudley, queen-maker and would-be scion of the Protestant ascendancy, whose delirious plan to supersede the legitimate Mary with the expedient Lady Jane Grey was always doomed to failure. It did, however, pave the way for arguably England's greatest ever queen, Elizabeth I.

QUEEN ELIZABETH I'S ACCESSION

La naturelle à si hault hault non bas

Le tard retour fera marris contens,

Le Recloing ne sera sans debatz

En empliant et pendant tout son temps.

The natural daughter, not low at all, is set
so very high

This late comeback will please the apologists

The secret will be much debated

Both in the filling, and during all of her tenure.

England's King Henry VIII married Spain's Catherine of Aragon (youngest surviving child of King Ferdinand and Queen Isabella) on the 11th June 1509. As well as suffering a number of miscarriages, Catherine bore Henry two short-lived sons and a longer-lived daughter, Mary, who became his heir – and as far as the Catholic Church was concerned, that was that (despite Catherine's formerly having been married to Henry's brother, Arthur, who had died a bare six months after the wedding). But Henry wanted a male heir, and commenced formal proceedings to have the marriage to Catherine annulled on account of the previous consummation with his brother (something which Catherine vehemently denied). When his mistress, Anne Boleyn, unexpectedly fell pregnant, Henry speeded up proceedings by dismantling the Roman Catholic Church in England and replacing it with a Protestant (and considerably more amenable) alternative. Thus, when Elizabeth (later to be Queen Elizabeth I) was born, the entire Catholic world believed her to be Henry's bastard daughter, with no technical rights to the throne of England whatsoever.

In fact the arguments and recriminations continued throughout Elizabeth's reign, culminating in the alliance of Spain and Portugal and in the creation of the massive Armada, designed to carry an invading army into the very heart of England, and secure her, once again, for Catholicism. The Armada was indirectly triggered by the following Papal Bull of 1570, which gives just some idea of the long-standing differences between the disputatious parties:

Elizabeth, the pretended queen of England, a slave of wickedness, lending thereunto a helping hand, with whom, as in a sanctuary, the most pernicious of all men have found a refuge. The very woman having seized on the kingdom, and monstrously usurping the supreme place of the Head of the Church in all England, and the chief authority and jurisdiction thereof, has again brought back the said kingdom into miserable destruction, which was then newly reduced to the Catholic faith and good fruits...

[*See also* 8/66 – 1566: The Holy *Imperium* & The *Potestas Absoluta*]

Summary

Deemed illegitimate by the Catholic Church, Queen Elizabeth I secured England for Protestantism via her navy's 1588 defeat of the Spanish Armada, and became one of its greatest ever monarchs.

TREATY OF CATEAU-CAMBRÉSIS

1559

6/58

Entre les deux monarques esloignés,

Lors que Sol par Selin clair perdue:

Simulté grande entre deux indignés

Qu'aux Isles et Sienne la liberté rendue.

Between the two distanced monarchs

When the clear sun is lost because of Selin

Great enmity between the two indignant ones

Thus liberty is restored to Siena and
the Islands.

Given Nostradamus's index date of 6/58, it is most likely that this quatrain refers to the 1559 Treaty of Cateau-Cambrésis, which finally put an end to nearly sixty years of warfare between the two great kingdoms (the 'two distanced monarchs') of France and Spain (respectively 'the sun', and Selene/Selin, the moon) – a dispute brought to crisis point by the Hapsburg/Valois War of 1547–59. Under the terms of the treaty, Siena was sold to Duke Cosimo de Medici (having been, to all intents and purposes, his since 1557), and Corsica ('the islands') was handed over to the Genoese.

The 'good news' of the end of the war was somewhat leavened by the death of King Henri II of France in a freak jousting accident. The accident occurred during the tournament called on to celebrate both the peace, and the series of complicated marriages that were contrived to cement its accord. Nostradamus's early fame rests almost completely on the fact that he predicted the death of Henri II a number of years before it happened, in his famous quatrain 1/35, which follows immediately after this.

SUMMARY

The Treaty of Cateau-Cambrésis marked the long desired end to the lengthy series of disputes and wars between France and Spain, concerning the political, military, religious, and trade dominance of the European mainland.

KING HENRI II OF FRANCE

10 JULY 1559

1/35

Le lion jeune le vieux surmontera,
En champ bellique par singulier duelle:
Dans caige d'or les yeux lui crevera,
Deux classes une, puis mourir, mort cruelle.

The young lion will overcome the old one

Hand to hand, on the field of combat

His eyes will burst in their golden helmet

Two breaks in one, followed by a
merciless death.

Published a full three years before the fateful death it foretold, this is the famous quatrain detailing the death, in a joust, of King Henri II of France. Despite repeated warnings from both Nostradamus, his queen, and his Italian court astrologer, Luca Gaurico, the virile forty-one-year-old king insisted on taking an active part in the three-day tournament arranged to celebrate the double marriages of his sister, Marguerite, to the Duke of Savoy, and of his eldest daughter, Elizabeth, to King Philip II of Spain, as agreed in the Treaty of Cateau-Cambrésis. [*See* 6/58 – 1559]

Galvanised by his success in the first two days of the jousting, Henri challenged Gabriel de Lorge, Count of Montgomery, and captain of his Scottish Guard, to ritual single combat on the third and final day of the tournament. They duly exchanged lances, leading to a tie. But Henri was not satisfied – he insisted on a second bout. Montgomery havered. The king, despite the entreaties of his wife, stood on his rights as a combatant. The joust took place. At the very last moment, sensing disaster, the thirty-five-year-old Montgomery tried to avoid the king's person, but his lance caught on the lip of Henri's helmet, splintering on his visor, and entering the king's right orbit and temple, just above the right eye.

Despite prompt treatment by Master Surgeon Ambroise Paré, and Philip II's great anatomist, Andreas Vesalius, Henri began to succumb to cerebral infection and cerebral trauma. Desperate to find a remedy for her husband's injury, his queen, Catherine de Medici, ordered four criminals to be beheaded, and broken truncheons to be forced into their right eyes 'at an appropriate angle' in order to ascertain the full extent of the king's wound. The cerebral trauma, however, had now caused Henri's left eye to become grotesquely swollen, even further mirroring Nostradamus's original prediction. Four days after the joust, and despite the best efforts of his wife and surgeons, the king became feverish, quickly followed by paralysis of the right side and lengthy convulsions. Henri died an agonising death six days later, on the 10th July 1559. He was buried in a cadaver tomb at the Basilica of St Denis, and his premature death undoubtedly changed the course of French and European history.

The crestfallen Montgomery, pardoned by the king on his deathbed, succumbed to the widowed queen's disfavour a full fifteen years after her husband's death. That, too, was predicted by Nostradamus, in quatrain 3/30, right down to the six armed men who kidnapped him, naked, from his bedroom, and hurried him to the Conciergerie prison, where this belated Protestant convert and survivor of the Massacre of the Huguenots conveniently died.

Summary

Refusing to listen to Nostradamus's repeated warnings that he would die in a joust, macho King Henri II of France is fatally injured during a tournament to celebrate the joint marriages of his daughter and sister, and the peace treaty of Cateau-Cambrésis. Henri's death was good news for Spain, England, Italy and Austria, and particularly good news for Nostradamus, whose divinatory fame it secured.

NOSTRADAMUS AND HIS BENEFACTRESS, CATHERINE DE MEDICI

DATE

1563

QUATRAIN

6/63

La Dame seule au regne demeurée

L'unic esteint premier au lict d'honneur:

Sept ans sera de douleur explorée,

Puis longue vie au regne par grand heur.

The widowed Lady will remain in the kingdom

Her only husband will die first on the field of honour

Seven years will be put aside for mourning

The realm will long endure in greatness.

On the 25th March 1552, on the occasion of a military expedition to Germany, Henri II declared his wife, Catherine de Medici, regent, either in his absence or in the event of his premature death. Seven years later, just as Nostradamus had predicted in 1/35 – 1559 [King Henri II Of France], Henri died in a freak accident whilst jousting – wearing, it is said, his mistress Diane de Poitiers' colours of black and white – and this foresight became reality.

According to novelist Honoré de Balzac, it was at that time customary for mourning queens to remain in their dead husband's bedchamber for forty days and nights with no light other than that of wax tapers. Catherine – although nominally devoted to her husband despite his many years of open dalliance with the seventeen-year-older-than-himself Diane (who had also been his father's mistress) – contrived to avoid this fate by removing the court from Paris to St Germain under the pretext of protecting her son from Protestant heretics. She did, however, adopt the motto *Lachrymae Hinc, Hinc Dolor* ('Thus the tears, thus the pain') as a sop to her dead husband's memory, together with various other grieving appurtenances during the seven-year mourning period. Oscar Wilde, in his *The Portrait Of Dorian Gray* (Chapter 11) describes one of them thus:

> Catherine de Medici had a mourning-bed made
> for her of black velvet powdered with crescents
> and suns. Its curtains were of damask, with leafy
> wreaths and garlands, figured upon a gold and
> silver ground, and fringed along the edges with

broideries of pearls, and it stood in a room hung
with rows of the queen's devices in cut black
velvet upon cloth of silver.

Not *too* inconvenient, then. The date 1563 refers to the end of
Catherine's son, Charles IX's, minority, when, in theory,
Catherine should have handed the power of the state over
to him – in practice, she dominated him during the entirety
of his reign. She did write him a famous letter in that year,
in which she lectured him (nominally via philosopher Michel
de Montaigne) on how he ought to comport himself:

> For I often heard the King your grandfather say
> that two things were necessary for the French to
> live in peace and love their King; keep them in
> high spirits, and occupied with some exercise or
> other..... For the French are so accustomed to
> exercise themselves, if there is no war, that if
> exercises are not provided they turn to things
> more dangerous.

The Royal French Realm, despite Nostradamus's *nostrum*
and Catherine's Confucian warnings, was to endure for only
a further 226 years.

Summary

Nostradamus (writing in 1557) placates Catherine de Medici
by prophesying what he feels that she would want, should
the death of her husband occur as foretold in 1/35 – 1559
[King Henri II Of France].

THE HOLY *IMPERIUM* &
THE *POTESTAS ABSOLUTA*

DATE

1566

QUATRAIN
8 / 66

Quand l'escriture D. M. trouvee,
Et cave antique à lampe descouverte,
Loy, Roy, et Prince Ulpian esprouvee,
Pavillon Royne et Duc sous la couverte.

When the words D. M. are found

And the ancient cave is discovered by lamplight

Law, king and prince will be tested by Ulpian

Both queen and duke are coated by the flag.

This is a complex quatrain, and I make no apology for going into it in some detail. The Roman jurist Ulpian (author of *De Officio Proconsulis*) maintained that there were two branches of the study of law, namely public (religion, priesthoods and magistracies) and private (in which towns were treated as private individuals) – as such he can fairly claim to be the first person to have postulated this fundamental divide, albeit with a clear subtext to his statement involving the clearing away of public law (together with the *ius naturale* and *ius gentium*) in favour of a very Roman concentration on private law. Ulpian maintained, too, that composite law did not apply to the emperor, and here we find ourselves moving closer to the actual meat of the quatrain, which deals with the concept of *imperium*, which presupposes that one only has power over someone lower in the hierarchy than oneself – a consul over a praetor or a magistrate, say, but not over another consul – whilst the emperor has power over just about everybody, and thus becomes the, de facto, office of last resort. This concept of *imperium* then finds itself melded (but still essentially in opposition) to that of *iurisdictio*, which embraces merely the formal administering of justice.

Ulpian's work incorporated his concept of the *potestas absoluta* (absolute power), triggered by his twin precepts *quod principi placuit legis habet vigorem*: i.e. that whatever pleases the emperor has the power of law – and also *princeps legibus solutus est*: i.e. that a prince is above the law. These themes duly found themselves echoed in a famous book of 1566 (*see* index date) by Jean Bodin, the *Methodus Ad Facilem Historiarum Cognitionem*, which also saw the beginning of Bodin's obsession with the nature of sovereignty, an obsession which found its truest expression in his *Les Six Livres De La République* (1576), in which he posits the question of just how many powers can a sovereign (or in the case of this quatrain, a pontiff) reasonably cede to others without ceasing to exercise his authority (it was anti-Justinian, therefore, in essence).

For Nostradamus's purposes, the publication of Bodin's *Methodus* in 1566 just happened to coincide with the election of Pope Pius V (otherwise known as the Dominican Michele – initials D. M.), a fundamentalist pope and former Supreme Inquisitor, who resisted Protestant theological incursions and effectively bent a lax, decadent and corrupt Catholic Church to his will. It was he who published the famous 27th April 1570 bull, *Regnans In Excelsis*, which effectively accused Queen Elizabeth I of England of heretical bastardy, and which strove to absolve all her subjects from any allegiance towards her [*see* 10/84 – 1558: Queen Elizabeth I's Accession, for a verbatim quote].

SUMMARY

Nostradamus is quite simply reiterating his belief that Holy Law should come higher up in the hierarchy than Royal Law, and he is quoting Ulpian, Bodin and the example of D. M. (Dominican Michele) to that very effect. Nostradamus firmly believed, of course, that the practice of religion equated with 'good news'.

THE GOOD NEWS
QUATRAINS

MARGARET FARNESE, DUCHESS OF PARMA

1567

2 / 67

Le blonde au nez forchu viendra commettre,
Par le duelle et chassera dehors:
Les exilés dedans fera remettre,
Aux lieux marins commettant les plus forts.

The blonde will become embroiled with the
hook-nosed one

Via a duel, and be driven out

The internal exiles will restore the status quo

They will commit their bravest to the sea.

The famous portrait of the Duke of Alva, by Titian, shows a hook-nosed and supremely self-important man, more than matched by his portrait by Anthony More (Antonio Moro), which shows, in addition, Alva's latent cruelty – this is a man that no one, in their right minds, would want to tangle with. But tangle with him Margaret of Parma did, over her right – through the belated acknowledgment of her legitimacy by her father, Charles V, and the wishes of her brother, Philip II – to be the regent of the Spanish Netherlands and representative of Catholic Spain's interests there. She, too, had her portrait painted by Anthony More, and it shows a powerfully single-minded blonde woman, standing, like a man, with one hand casually supported on a velvet covered chaise. By calling her *le blonde* (blonde with an e is usually feminine, and carries a feminine prefix – blonde also carries with it the connotation of being difficult to please), Nostradamus was shrewdly pointing up just those masculine qualities for which she was famous.

But the Spanish Netherlands were in a long-term state of revolt, thanks to high taxes, the Inquisition, and the rejection of Catholicism in favour of Calvinism by a significant proportion of the Dutch population – and Margaret had been accorded no troops by Philip with which to reinforce Spanish hegemony over the by now disenchanted minor nobility. Margaret tried her best to stem the flood by suspending all religious decrees, but the Iconoclastic Riots broke out in 1566, followed by an armed uprising under Count Brederode, which was, though, soon crushed by the use of mercenaries.

Philip was fearful, however, of losing his privileged access to the Antwerp bullion markets through which the rich profits from Spain's New World adventures were funnelled, so in 1567 he sent in the notorious Duke of Alva, with 9,000 men, to rectify the situation – they arrived in August, charged with restoring order and levying taxes. Alva immediately deposed Margaret, who rather reluctantly retired to her husband's estates in Italy, and he then began a notorious reign of terror (nicknamed the Council of Blood), in which more than 9,000 men were condemned, with 1,000 immediate executions and exiles. His conduct, though effective in the short term, would ultimately lead to the Netherlands' total disenchantment with Spain, symbolised by the formation of the 'Sea Beggars' (*see* line 4), consisting of refugees from the north of the Netherlands (allied to the French Huguenots, under Coligny), who harried the Spanish shipping unmercifully, eventually creating a mini-state for themselves based around Flushing and Brill.

Summary

Good news for religiously tolerant Holland, in that Margaret of Parma's deposition as regent by the Duke of Alva indirectly led to the formation of the Netherlands as a Free State, and to its long-standing supremacy as a trading nation.

THE HUGUENOTS & THE SECOND WAR OF RELIGION

Une nouvelle secte de Philosophes

Mesprisant mort, or, honneurs et richesses,

Des monts Germains ne seront limitrophes:

A les ensuivre auront appuy et presses.

A new philosophical sect

Disdaining death, gold, honours and riches

They will not confine themselves within the borders of the German Alps

It follows that they will not lack for either support or adherents.

The tricky words here are *Germain*, meaning closely related to (as in first cousins, descending from an uncle or aunt) and *limitrophes*, meaning bordering on or contiguous to – with difficulty, therefore, we come to 'At one with the faraway mountains' or, if taken metaphorically, 'They will not confine themselves within the borders of the German Alps'. Given the index date of 67, which coincides with the beginning, on the 29th September 1567, of the Second War of Religion in France, this commentator at least considers it likely that the *cousins Germains* (first cousins) mentioned in line 3 relate to the Huguenots, many of whom were intimately related to the French Catholics whom they were constrained, on dogmatic (ergo 'philosophical' grounds), to fight. When one adds to this the fact that the 'new philosophical sect' of Protestantism which fuelled the Huguenots – who termed themselves the Protestant Reformed Church of France, and whose name had first arisen a mere seven years before as a direct result of the Amboise plot of 1560 in which 1,200 Protestants were hung on iron hooks outside the Chateau d'Amboise – actually stemmed from just across the 'German Alps', then the reading is surely reinforced. The actual word *Huguenot* probably originated from the *Eid Genossen* or 'oath fellows' (which in Flemish was transposed to *Huis Genooten*, or 'house fellows'), and which consisted of Bible students from the Swiss and German borders, who gathered together at each others' houses, under oath of secrecy, to study the words and biblical commentaries of the Luther-influenced (and recently deceased) Jean Chauvin (John Calvin).

Anyway, when the Prince de Condé and Gaspard de Coligny [*see* next quatrain] failed in their attempt to capture King Charles IX and his mother, Catherine de Medici, at Meaux, on the 29th September 1567, the scene was set for another lengthy stand-off between the warring religious parties, exemplified by the 10th November 1567's Battle of St-Denis, in which 16,000 Catholic Royalists attacked 3,500 Huguenots, led by the Prince de Condé. Astonishingly, the Huguenots held the Catholics off for some little time, mortally wounding their (male) leader, Anne, Duke of Montmorency, who died two days later, in Paris. A whimsical and initially reluctant Charles IX, belatedly galvanised into action by his mother, Catherine de Medici, later oversaw the 1572 St Bartholomew's Day Massacre of French Huguenots – he died, however, a mere two years later, an old man at twenty-four, racked by nightmares and diabolical visions.

Summary

Nostradamus describes John Calvin's virile new philosophy of Protestantism, and the French Wars of Religion which stemmed from his teachings, and which were to culminate in the notorious St Bartholomew's Day Massacre of 1572, which finally secured France (and here's the good news as far as Nostradamus is concerned) for Catholicism.

GASPARD DE COLIGNY

13 MARCH 1569

3/69

Grand excercite conduict par jouvenceau,
Se viendra rendre aux mains des ennemis:
Mais le vieillard nay au demi pourceau,
Fera Chalon et Mascon estre amis.

A great army led by a young man

Will surrender to the enemy

But the old man born to the half pig

Will cause Chalon and Macon to become
friends.

The thirty-nine-year-old Louis de Bourbon, Prince de Condé, lost his life at the Battle of Jarnac in 1569, when the Catholic forces, under Henry, Duke of Anjou, defeated the Protestant Huguenot forces he was commanding. This led directly to the regrouped Huguenots electing Henri de Bourbon, Duke of Vendôme (later Henri IV of France), as their titular new leader, with the fifty-year-old Admiral Gaspard de Coligny seconding him as military commander and sole leader of the Protestant armies. It is Coligny, therefore, later to die during the 1572 Massacre of the Huguenots, who we must assume is the old man (fifty was a goodly age in those days) born to the half pig. So why half pig? I would like to think that Nostradamus was making a pun on the name of Coligny's brother, François, Seigneur d'Andelot (an *andouillette* is a small sausage made out of the bowels or chitterlings of a pig) – for François was the person directly responsible for recruiting Coligny to the Huguenot cause. Either way, it is an elegant quatrain, covering a subject which would have both worried and fascinated Nostradamus in the run-up to his death in 1566.

SUMMARY

The death of the young Louis de Bourbon, and his replacement at the head of the Huguenot forces by the noble and admired Admiral Gaspard de Coligny.

THE CASKET LETTERS

Lettres trouvees de la roine les coffres,
Point de subscrit sans aucun nom d'hauteur
Par la police seront caché les offres,
Qu'on ne scaura qui sera l'amateur.

Letters attributed to the queen are found in a casket

They bear neither signature nor author's name

The government conceals the offers within them

So that no one will know who is responsible.

It is at least conceivable that Nostradamus actually met the fourteen-year-old Mary Queen of Scots when he found himself summoned by Catherine de Medici to appear at the French court in 1556. Catherine was to become Mary's mother-in-law in 1558, through the marriage to Mary of her son, the Dauphin (later François II). The marriage was short-lived, thanks to François's death only seventeen months after that of his father, Henri II [*see 1/35 – 1559: King Henri II Of France*]. François died of a purported ear infection, a misadventure which led directly to Mary's return to Scotland and to the tragic chain of events which followed, and which were to include the episode of the so-called 'casket letters'. These letters, appearing as if from nowhere, were used in evidence in the formal inquiry Mary underwent for the alleged murder of her second husband, Lord Darnley (heir to the Earl of Lennox), and her half-first cousin.

Most subsequent commentators now view these letters as forgeries, designed to implicate the recently abdicated Mary in the murder of her husband – and even Elizabeth I, who bore Mary considerable ill-will, chose eventually to ignore them, whilst retaining Mary in 'protective custody' for the next eighteen years, until her execution for treason in 1587.

SUMMARY

A series of grammatically poor letters (Mary was a fluent French speaker), which appeared to implicate Mary Queen of Scots in the murder of her second husband, Lord Darnley. Somewhat surprisingly, in the circumstances, Mary found herself exonerated.

END OF FRANCE'S FIFTH WAR OF RELIGION

1576

3/76

En Germanie naistront diverses sectes,
S'approchans fort de l'heureux paganisme,
Le coeur captif et petites receptes,
Feront retour à payer le vray disme.

Various sects will be born in Germany

Closely resembling happy paganism

The captive heart and small dividends

Will return them to paying the true tithe.

One might at first be tempted to assume that this is simply a generalised hope on Nostradamus's part that after his death the Protestant sects originating from 'the German alps' [*see* 3/67 – 1567: The Huguenots & The Second War Of Religion] are finally constrained to see sense and return to the folds – and to the coffers – of the Catholic mother Church. But the index date of 76 is so specific, and would appear to refer to so precise a thing, that more begs to be read into the quatrain.

The year 1576 (a mere four years after the appalling Massacre of the Huguenots in Paris) saw the end of France's Fifth War of Religion, which culminated in a definite Huguenot advance, epitomised by the right granted to all Protestants to garrison eight strongholds, and to worship freely in all places throughout France, save only in Paris. The Huguenots had by this time effectively created a semi-autonomous state in the Languedoc area of southern France, in direct defiance of the French crown. The end of the Fifth War in 1576 saw them also accorded, via the Treaty of Monsieur, a series of chambers, adjoining every *parlement* (general assembly), which were to be known as *chambres-mi-parties*, and which were specifically for use in cases of Protestant litigation.

These – on the face of them rather unlikely – concessions, granted by Henri III, were secretly designed to control the power of the mighty Guise family, but they only succeeded in inflaming the Guises further, and a Sixth, Seventh, Eighth and Ninth War of Religion, culminating in the 1598 Edict of Nantes and the restitution of the Treaty of Cateau-

Cambrésis (in favour of the Huguenots), was the somewhat inevitable outcome.

Summary

A decidedly wishful quatrain in which Nostradamus appears to suggest that the Huguenots will eventually see the foolishness of their ways and return to the mother Church. The good news (at least as far as the Catholic Nostradamus is concerned) is that this did indeed happen in the case of Henri IV of Navarre, who felt that Paris was, indeed, 'surely worth a mass' [*see* 4/93 – 1593: Good King Henry Of Navarre].

MARY QUEEN OF SCOTS

8 FEBRUARY 1587

10/19

Jour que sera par roine saluee,

Le jour apres le salut, la priere,

Le compte fait raison et valbuee,

Par avant humbles oncques ne feut si fiere.

One day she will be acknowledged as a queen

The very next day she will pray

The reckoning is a right and a good one

Above all humble, never was there one so proud.

A direct follow-on to 8/23 – 1569 [The Casket Letters], the Catholic Nostradamus would most probably have viewed the execution of Mary Queen of Scots by the Protestant Elizabeth I as martyrdom at best, and *lèse majesté* at worst. Mary was only told of her execution at dinner the night before it was due to take place, and therefore had very little time to write letters, make her will, and pray. She was, in addition, denied the comfort of her own chaplain and the last Sacrament, her warders being most insistent (for obvious reasons) that she avail herself of a Protestant minister instead.

The execution itself was appallingly (and quite possibly purposely) botched, in that an anointed queen required three blows from the headsman (the first one striking her agonisingly on the shoulder) before the decapitation was complete. Just before the beheading, Mary had thrown off her black cloak to reveal a deep-red dress, the traditional liturgical colour symbolising martyrdom in the Catholic Church, and from amongst whose folds her lapdog, covered in its mistress's blood, belatedly ran. Mary's remains were later embalmed and sealed in an above-ground lead casket to prevent the taking of relics.

Although not formally canonised by the Roman Catholic Church, many Catholics consider Mary a martyr in the Church's cause, and this, and only this aspect of the whole affair, may, in retrospect, be considered 'good news'.

Summary

The execution of Mary Queen of Scots was a direct precursor of the disastrous invasion of England by the Spanish Armada in 1588, triggered by Pope Sixtus V's granting of formal papal authority to overthrow Queen Elizabeth I for regicide. England's unexpected victory led directly to the formation of its largely benevolent empire, and indirectly to the eventual liberation of the Americas from colonial rule.

SHAH ABBAS THE GREAT

1590

3/90

Le grand Satyre et Tigre d'Hyrcanie,
Don presente à ceux de l'Ocean:
Le chef de classe istra de Carmanie
Qui prendra terre au Tyrren Phocean.

The great Satyr and tiger (Tigris) of Hyrcania

A gift presented to those of the Ocean

The leader of the fleet will come from Carmania

He will make landfall at Tyrren Phocea.

Names are always problematical in Nostradamus, as they may mean a number of things – let's go through the list at our leisure, therefore. Both Hyrcania and Carmania were provinces of the old Persian empire, Hyrcania being situated between the Caspian Sea (known in ancient times as the Hyrcanian Ocean) and the present-day Elborz mountains, whilst Carmania, originally part of the Achaemenid Empire, is also situated in modern-day Iran, abutting on the Persian Gulf at Bandār-e-Abbas. Phocea (known as the mother of Marseilles, because colonists from the ancient Greek town were its founders), was situated near Smyrna (the modern Izmir, in Turkey), two seas away (the Aegean and the Adriatic) from Italy's Tyrrhenian Sea ('Tyrren'), and is principally known for the appalling massacre, in 1914, of its Christian inhabitants by the Turks.

One wonders, therefore, thanks to the index date of 90, whether Nostradamus is not alluding to the 1590 agreement in which the nineteen-year-old Shah Abbas I of Persia finally made peace with the Ottomans, all the better to pursue his campaign against Abdullah II's Uzbeks, who had moved into southern Turkmenistan and northeastern Iran (abutting on Hyrcania)? Could Shah Abbas the Great be the 'great Satyr and tiger of Hyrcania' therefore? After all, Abbas was renowned for having disinherited and imprisoned his own father, aged only seventeen, and later for killing his principal ally, Morshed Gholi Ostajlou, and even for disposing of his eldest son, Safi Mirza, before going on to become the most eminent ruler of the Safavid dynasty. In 1615 he massacred 60,000 Georgians, and transplanted 100,000 others, before taking Baghdad in 1623. In a further echo of the quatrain, 1622 saw Abbas capturing the island of Hormuz from the Portuguese, and transferring all of its trade to the town of Bander Abbas, home (you've guessed it – *see above*) of the ancient world's Carmania. Abbas, however, unlike the Turks in 1914, was by and large renowned for his tolerance of his Christian subjects in Armenia. When he finally died in 1629, his empire stretched from the Tigris to the Indus, turning the end of Nostradamus's line 1, the *'Tigre d'Hyrcanie'*, into a sublime pun – for *Tigre* is the French word for the Tigris.

One final note: the 'leader of the fleet' mentioned in line 3 is no doubt the adventurer Sir Robert Shirley, whom Abbas later sent to Italy, Spain and England (making 'landfall at Tyrrhen') as part of a successful diplomatic effort aimed at creating a compact with which to counter the influence of the Ottomans.

Summary

A sublime quatrain in which Nostradamus puns his way into the life of Persia's Shah Abbas The Great, leaching out the key events throughout his empire-making reign.

SIR RICHARD GRENVILLE

10/11 SEPTEMBER 1591

6/91

Du conducteur de la guerre navale,
Rouge effrené, severe horrible grippe,
Captif eschappé de l'aisné dans la basle:
Quant il naistra du grand un filz Agrippe.

This is a tale of a naval commander

A man of unbridled temper, and austere, dreadful whims

A bullet in the groin secures his escape from captivity

Born of a great man, he is an Agrippan son.

Sir Richard Grenville (1541–91) came from a long line of great naval men, which included his father, Sir Roger Grenville, who commanded the ill-fated *Mary Rose*, and his grandfather, Sir Richard Grenville, who was appointed Marshal of Calais under King Henry VIII. A man of uncertain temper – a letter from Ralph Lane to Sir Francis Walsingham in 1585 describes him as 'of intolerable pride and insatiable ambition' and a memorandum from Jan Huygen Linschoten portrays him as 'very unquiet in his mind and greatly affected to war... of nature very severe, so that his own people hated him for his fierceness and spoke very hardly of him' – Grenville was made vice-admiral and second-in-command of an important naval expedition to the Azores in 1591.

Given the 500-ton, 250-man *Revenge* as his flagship, he and the *Revenge*'s fifteen sister ships gave chase to a fleet of fifty-three Spanish ships of the line. With a goodly proportion of his crew still stranded on land, sick with fever and the scurvy, Grenville was in no real condition to offer battle. Acting under what has sometimes been construed as a 'false sense of honour' – a criticism that was also made by members of the Roman Senate about naval crown winner Marcus Vipsanius 'Agrippa' (63 BC–12 BC), and which even contributed to the eventual boycott of his funeral games – Grenville, with angry voice and gesture, made clear his intention of passing directly through the Spanish fleet to retrieve his sick men.

The inevitable happened. Falling under the lee canvas of that great Spanish galleon, the *San Felipe*, the *Revenge* suddenly found herself becalmed. Boarded by the *San Felipe*'s crew, Grenville and his 150 men fought a gallant 15-hour hand-to-hand battle against up to 5,000 Spaniards and 15 of their ships, only surrendering (against Grenville's express orders) when just 20 wounded men were left alive. The *Revenge*'s admiral, mortally wounded by a musket ball ('a bullet in the groin'), was taken captive aboard the Spanish flagship *San Pablo*, where he died, a few days later, just as Nostradamus describes in line 3.

Tennyson has this to say of Grenville, in his 1880 poem, *The Revenge*:

> But he rose upon their decks and he cried:
> 'I have fought for Queen and Faith like a valiant
> man and true.
> I have only done my duty as a man is bound to
> do.
> With a joyful spirit I, Sir Richard Grenville, die!'
> And he fell upon their decks and he died.

Summary

Although a tragedy in the strictest sense of the word, Sir Richard Grenville's gallant death aboard the *Revenge* provided a magnificent moral victory for the British in their propaganda war against the abuse of Spanish sea power. James Anthony Froude, in his *Short Studies*, describes it thus: 'It dealt a more deadly blow upon their fame and moral strength than the destruction of the Armada itself, and in the direct results which arose from it, it was scarcely less disastrous to them.'

GOOD KING HENRY OF NAVARRE

1593

4/93

Un serpent veu proche du lict royal,

Sera par dame, nuict chiens n'abayeront:

Lors naistre en France un Prince tant royal,

Du ciel venu tous les Princes verront.

A serpent is seen close to the royal bed

This will be by the lady, at night, and the dogs will not bark

Upon which there will be born in France a prince so regal

That other princes will see him as descended from heaven.

This, is not an easy quatrain to disassemble, as it is largely couched in metaphorical, rather than in literal language: i.e. 'the serpent', 'the royal bed', 'the dogs (who) will not bark', and 'descended from heaven'. All of these pointers are – at least according to the medieval conventions surrounding such conceits – designed to be taken as signs or signifiers, emblematic of tendencies rather than of specific outcomes. One thing we do know is that Nostradamus interested himself in the young Henri de Navarre, son-in-law of his patroness, Catherine de Medici, through his marriage to her daughter, the now cinematically famous *La Reine Margot*. This circumstance, taken with the index date of 93 (which coincides with a pivotal moment in Henri's reign during which he was, quite literally, reborn) would tend to suggest that such a reading is firmly anchored in fact.

For the year 1593 marked the true beginning of the Bourbon dynasty, triggered by Henri's somewhat reluctant espousal of the Catholic faith, without which his time on the throne might have been even more truncated than it actually was (he was assassinated, aged fifty-seven, by a rabid Catholic, François Ravaillac, possibly at the instigation of his second wife, Marie de Medici). His famous words – and the words that, according to the Catholic League, consti-tuted his spiritual rebirth, finally entitling him to the throne of France – were '*Paris vaut bien une messe*' ('Paris is surely worth a mass'). The 'lady, at night' must therefore be Henri's beloved mistress, Gabrielle d'Estrées (by whom he had numerous children), who encouraged him to take the Catholic pledge; 'the 'serpent' is either his mother-in-law,

Catherine de Medici, whose natal line Henri IV effectively usurped, or his second wife Marie de Medici, who may or may not have engineered his death, fatally changing the history of France in the process; the 'non-barking dogs' must then be the Catholic League, created by Henri de Guise, in 1576, in order to extirpate the Protestant faith from France.

Arguably France's most popular ever king, Henri IV both cared for his people – 'If God allows me life, I will make sure that every worker in my kingdom has at least enough money to afford a chicken in his pot every Sunday' – and practised a quite anti-Valois religious tolerance (the 1598 Edict of Nantes, which afforded considerable protection to French Huguenots). He also believed in ruling with 'a weapon in his hand and with his arse in the saddle' – this made of him a quite uncharacteristic French monarch, and the 'prince among princes' that Nostradamus so effectively describes.

Summary

A quatrain lauding Good King Henry of Navarre, arguably France's greatest ever king, and something of a religious pragmatist. He reconverted to Catholicism, despite his Huguenot convictions, the better to secure the French realm for the Bourbons and to ensure its religious and political unity.

GUSTAVUS II ADOLPHUS 'THE GREAT' OF SWEDEN

9 DECEMBER 1596

3/94

De cinq cent ans plus compte lon tiendra
Celuy qu'estoit l'ornement de son temps:
Puis à un coup grand clarté donrra
Que par ce siecle les rendra trescontens.

For a calculation of five hundred years more
they will hold him

He who was the ornament of his age

Then, all of a sudden, great clarity will prevail

Which, in that century, will please them.

For some reason the figure given in this quatrain of 'five hundred years' has obsessed Nostradamian scholars for most of its (albeit notional) time. Did Nostradamus mean lunar years or calendar years? And from when was he counting? From his birth? From his death (as if!)? Lengthy careers have been based on less...

It behoves us to approach the question from a different direction (or so it seems to me), along the lines of identifying the 'ornament of his age' by means of the index date, and calculating on from there. For instance, 1594 gives us the coronation of King Henri IV of France, a man who was certainly considered a great ornament to both France and to universal tolerance. However it also marks the birth of the Protestant King Gustavus II Adolphus of Sweden, known as 'the Great', and idolised by both Napoleon Bonaparte and Carl von Clausewitz as one of the greatest generals of all time. Gustavus was the most democratic of military leaders, treating even the lowliest of his soldiers (not to mention his famous musketeers) with both fairness and dignity. Often to be seen at the head of his cuirassiers during cavalry charges, he was wounded on a number of occasions, taking musket balls to the neck, the throat, and the trunk. Because of one such wound he had a special leather suit of armour designed for him which was guaranteed not to irritate his neck and spine during his more spirited encounters with the enemy.

Fond of travelling incognito throughout Europe under the pseudonym of Captain Gars (*Gustavus Adolphus Rex Sueciae*), Gustav finally met his comeuppance at the Battle of

Lützen, in 1632, when he was separated from his men in the mist, during a cavalry charge, and brought down by the enemy (in this case the Holy Roman Empire and the Catholic German States, under Albrecht von Wallenstein). Alerted to his untimely death (he was only thirty-seven), the Swedish Riksdag of the Estates went to the unprecedented lengths of according him the perpetual accolade of 'the Great' – a signal honour that has never been repeated.

SUMMARY

A paean to the excellent King Gustavus II Adolphus of Sweden, who has his very own flag day of 6th November, on which only one particular pastry, with a chocolate medallion of the king set into it, is customarily sold.

THE BRITISH EMPIRE I

Le grand empire sera par Angleterre,

Le pempotam des ans plus de trois cens:

Grandes copies passer par mer et terre,

Les Lusitains n'en seront pas contens.

The greatest empire will be that of England

Plenipotentiary for more than three hundred years

Vast armies will move across sea and land

The Lusitanians will not be best pleased.

This may, on the surface, seem a straightforward quatrain – England to have the greatest of all empires. So what's new about that? But this quatrain was published in Lyons, by Benoit Rigaud, in 1568, at a time when England, under its monarch Elizabeth I, was still a relatively minor power (although it was reportedly first printed in 1558, implying that the quatrain was actually written even marginally before Elizabeth's accession to the throne). Suffice it to say that the quatrain is magnificently prescient, with an index date of 1600 giving us the granting of a royal charter by Queen Elizabeth I to the British East India Company, acknowledged by many as the world's first multinational corporation, and destined to be the symbolic and commercial bedrock of empire for the next 258 years.

In line 4 Nostradamus mentions that 'the Lusitanians will not be best pleased' by this anticipated train of events. Lusitania was a Roman province, constituted by the emperor Augustus, circa 5 AD, which incorporated much of what is now central Portugal and western Spain – and in the sixteenth century, expansionist Portugal, together with imperial Spain, represented the two greatest competitors to Britain's colonial ambitions during the early years of the formation of the British Empire. With the benefit of a hindsight Nostradamus did not share, we now know that both Catholic Iberian empires would ally themselves, in the form of the 1588 Spanish Armada, in what was designed to be a permanent tooth-drawing operation against the English Protestant upstarts. In the event, the Armada failed dismally in its object, leaving the way open for Britain's ensuing mastery of the seas, and the gradual construction of its mighty overseas empire.

Despite numerous ups and downs during its 'more than three hundred years' of history, by 1921 the British Empire incorporated a quarter of the world's population (i.e. up to 570 million dependent subjects), and a quarter of the world's landmass (i.e. up to 14.3 million square miles of potential land area). Termed the empire upon which the sun never set, it was certainly true that at any given time the sun would be shining on at least one of Britain's vast panoply of overseas territories.

Summary

Nostradamus correctly anticipates the full extent of the British Empire (the most comprehensive, and arguably the most benevolent, in world history) many years before its formal inception. [*See also* 10/42 – 1642/1942: The British Empire II]

THE SIEGE OF OSAKA

1615

7 / 15

Devant cité de l'insubre contree,

Sept ans sera le siege devant mis:

Le tres grand Roi y fera son entree,

Cité, puis libre hors de ses ennemis.

In front of the city of the insubordinate region

A siege will be laid for seven years

The very great king will make his entrance there

The city will then be free, its enemies outside.

It is very hard to envisage a seven-year siege (outside Homeric literature), so let us concentrate instead on the index date of 15, and see what emerges. The most likely contender for the 'city of the insubordinate region' must therefore be the November 1614 to June 1615 Siege of Osaka, by (the nominally retired) Shogun Tokugawa Ieyasu, which cemented the power of the Tokugawa Shogunate of Japan for the next 253 years, sealing Japan off from outside interference ('its enemies outside') and laying the basis for the destruction of all residual Christian influence that culminated in 3/38 – 1638 [The Shimabara Rebellion].

Rebuilt by the Toyotomi clan in 1614, Osaka stood as a brazen reminder to Ieyasu that all authority did not lie in his hands, or in the hands of Emperor Go-Yōzei, 'the very great king', and Japan's 107th imperial ruler, whom he nominally represented. Galvanised by the protection Osaka afforded him, the young Toyotomi Hideyori (son of the famous but lowly-born warlord Hideyoshi), began recruiting Ronin (samurai with no master) to his flag. By November, Ieyasu decided that enough was enough, and after a few preliminary skirmishes, he laid siege to Osaka on the 4th December with a force consisting of 194,000 men. The siege was only partially successful, and resulted in a temporary backdown by Hideyori, who expediently agreed to fill in Osaka's moat.

Hideyori was back to his old tricks again by the next April, however, forcing Ieyasu to return for a second bite at the Osaka cherry. This time he was entirely successful, and Hideyori committed seppuku (ritual suicide) as the castle burnt down around him. Hideyori's wife (who happened to be Ieyasu's granddaughter) was spared from the slaughter, but her infant son Kunimatsu (Hideyori's heir) was expediently murdered, as was his mother (Hideyoshi's widow), and any of the castle's defenders who were unfortunate enough to fall into Ieyasu's hands – their heads were later attached to planks of wood and exhibited on the Fushimi/Kyoto road for all to see.

Summary

Ieyasu's victory at Osaka cemented the power of the Tokugawa shogunate, sealing Japan off from outside interference and laying the foundations for the destruction, once and for all, of any residual Christian influence. Japan was to live in peace for much of the next 253 years.

KING JAMES I & VI

1617

7 / 17

Le prince rare de pitié et clemence,
Viendra changer par mort grand cognoissance
Par grand repos le regne travaillé,
Lors que le grand tost sera estrillé.

The singular prince, full of pity and clemency

Will change, gaining great knowledge
through death

The kingdom will be worked at in tranquillity

So long as the great man's back is rubbed.

A rather nice comment on power, this, with the vanity of kings neatly juxtaposed with their potential wisdom (one is reminded of Confucius). The year is 1617, of course, with James I of England and Ireland (and VI of Scotland) on the throne. Accounted the most intellectually accomplished king since Alfred the Great, James was also a bit of an idiot when it came to favouritism, and was accounted by some 'the wisest fool in Christendom' (he even wrote a well-intentioned treatise on witchcraft and demonology, which resulted in hundreds of unnecessary deaths – not to mention his somewhat hypocritical reaffirmation of the Buggery Act of 1533).

The year 1617 also saw James begin the process which made his favourite, George Villiers, into the Duke of Buckingham (titles were routinely bought and sold during James's reign) – something of a mistake, in retrospect, and a tribute to the sycophancy Nostradamus describes in line 4 with 'so long as the great man's back is rubbed' (a *double entendre*, if ever there was one). It also led to some wit penning the following: 'Elizabeth was King: now James is Queen.' James rather bravely defended his friendship with Villiers ('the most beautiful man in Europe') to the Privy Council that same year, using the following words:

> I, James, am neither a god nor an angel, but a
> man like any other. Therefore I act like a man
> and confess to loving those dear to me more
> than other men. You may be sure that I love the
> Earl of Buckingham more than anyone else, and

more than you who are here assembled. I wish to speak in my own behalf and not to have it thought to be a defect, for Jesus Christ did the same, and therefore I cannot be blamed. Christ had John, and I have George.

Despite the potentially explosive issue of James's homosexuality, his reign, by and large, was a peaceful one, during which culture of all sorts flourished, and which saw some of William Shakespeare and Francis Bacon's greatest works – not to mention the publication of the enormously influential and mellifluously euphonic Authorised Version of the Bible.

Summary

One of the few disguised mentions of homosexuality in the quatrains (*estrillé/étriller* means to be curried, beaten or rubbed, and was a polite medieval euphemism for buggery). Nostradamus seems to approve of James, by and large, even though he obviously thinks him an idiot.

THE EDICT FOR THE RESTITUTION OF CHURCH PROPERTY

1629

8 / 29

Au quart pillier lon sacre à Saturne.

Par tremblant terre et deluge fendu

Soubz l'edifice Saturnin trouvee urne,

D'or Capion ravy et puis rendu.

The fourth pillar is sacred to Saturn

Earthquake and flood cleave it in two

Under the Saturnine structure an urn is found

The gold is carried away by a two faced man,
and then returned.

Capion in line 4 gives us a happy juxtaposition between the word *capon*, meaning a double-faced or sly fellow in Old French, and the Roman Quintus Servilius Caepio, Proconsul of Cisalpine Gaul in 105 BC, who sacked Toulouse's temples of the equivalent of 50,000 15lb-bars of gold and 10,000 15lb-bars of silver. The 'two-faced' Caepio duly sent the gold back to his masters in Rome but, surprise, surprise, only the silver ever made it home; the gold being regrettably stolen en route by a gang of miscreants, allegedly hired by – you've guessed it – Caepio himself. Caepio received his comeuppance, however, when he managed to 'lose' an entire Roman army in battle against the Germans (the Cimbri and Teutoni), during the Battle of Arausio that same year. He was tried for the 'loss of an army' by the Tribune of the Plebs, exiled for life, and fined 15,000 talents of gold. As 15,000 talents is the equivalent of about 825,000lbs of the stuff, it could reasonably be said that the gold was, as Nostradamus correctly opines, returned (and with interest).

Readers may rightly say that this brings us no nearer to a more modern rendition of the quatrain, but the index date of 29 is of definite help here, for it pinpoints the 29th March 1629, the day on which Albrecht von Wallenstein began enforcing the German Edict for the Restitution Of Church Property, an edict which afforded the Catholic Church redress for the enforced secularisation of all Church property that had occurred between that date, 1629, and the 1555 Peace of Augsburg – a treaty which had effectively ended the Schmalkaldic Wars between the Holy Roman Empire and France, finally allowing German princes to choose freely between Lutheranism and Catholicism (*cuius regio, eius religio* – effectively, 'in the prince's land, the prince's religion').

Summary

Nostradamus compares the sacking of the temples at Toulouse in 105 with the 1555 Treaty of Augsburg – in both cases the effects were, in some ways at least, subsequently reversed, by means of the partial or complete restitution of the encumbered or stolen property.

THE SHIMABARA REBELLION

La gent Gauloise et nation estrange,

Outre les monts, morts prins et profligez

Au mois contraire et proche de vendange,

Par les Seigneurs en accord redigés.

French people and those of a strange nation

A prince is overcome and killed beyond
the mountains

Six months later, close to harvest time

The great ones draw up a peace agreement.

By 'strange' nation, Nostradamus is implying a nation of people foreign to European ways. In this case, given the index date of the quatrain, we are led to the Japanese, and to the great Shimabara rebellion of 1637/1638, which ultimately paved the way for ten generations (200 years) of continuous peace during the Edo period – an era in which Japan fought no major battles, and during which most samurai were never called upon to use their swords in any other than a ceremonial manner.

The rebellion was triggered by the teachings of French and Portuguese Jesuits (a movement whose inception dated back to the arrival of the University of Paris educated Francis Xavier in Japan in 1549, and whose *raison d'être* was reinforced by the crucifixion of the twenty-six Japanese martyrs at Nagasaki, on the 5th February 1597). In the region of 23,000 peasants and ronin (leaderless samurai) joined forces against their daimyo, Matsukura Shigeharu, and held out throughout the winter, taking as their base Shimabara Castle and the fortress of Hara. Their leader, Amakusa Shiro (a.k.a. Masuda Tokisada), who had proclaimed himself the fourth son of heaven (as foretold, apparently, by Francis Xavier), was later killed and beheaded, with his head spitted on a pike in Nagasaki as a warning to other turncoats and iconoclasts [*see* 7/15 – 1615: The Siege Of Osaka] .

SUMMARY

Christian Japanese peasants, with the support of French and Portuguese Jesuits, rise up against their daimyo in an effort to have their tax burden reduced. The rebel army holds out for nearly six months before it is beaten, and its leader, and 37,000 of his supporters, are beheaded. Having rid itself of foreign influences, Japan then benefits from nearly 200 years of largely uninterrupted peace.

THE BRITISH EMPIRE II

QUATRAIN
10/42

Le regne humain d'Anglique geniture,
Fera son regne paix union tenir,
Captive guerre demi de sa closture,
Long temps la paix leur fera maintenir.

The humane reign will come from England

It will hold in peace and union

Half of what it encloses will have been captured
by war

For a long time they will maintain the peace.

It's surprising how many of Nostradamus's quatrains deal with England, and English history. Given the tenor of 10/100 – 1600 [The British Empire I], it is clear that Nostradamus suspected that Britain, and not France, would end up by dominating the world for more than 300 years. Here, he extends and broadens that prediction, giving us 42 as his index date. This presents us with a dilemma, for both 1642 and 1942 represent critical dates in the formation and eventual dissolution of the British Empire.

Firstly, 1642 – a crucial year which marked the formal beginnings of the First English Civil War. On the 4th January King Charles I tried to arrest five members of the Long Parliament, but only succeeded in further exacerbating the gulf between king and legislature; in July, he besieged Hull, in an unsuccessful attempt to gain control of its arsenal; on the 22nd August the king formally raised his battle standard over Nottingham Castle, thereby declaring war on his own Parliament; and finally, on the 23rd October, the Battle of Edgehill became the first pitched battle in the Civil War, in which Charles, through an excess of caution, failed to follow up his critical advantage and take London, leading to a further three years of warfare. The events of 1642 were to lead directly to Charles's overthrow and eventual execution, on Tuesday 30th January 1649, and, indirectly, via the eventual restitution of the Stuarts in the form of Charles II, to the formal beginnings of the British Empire.

The year 1942, on the other hand, marked what might be seen, in retrospect, as the turning point, or fulcrum, of the United States/British axis of power. It was in that period that the British were expelled from Burma, Malaya and Singapore by the Japanese; in which the 'Quit India' resolution was passed by the Bombay section of the All India Congress Committee; and in which Britain only partially redeemed itself during the Second Battle of El Alamein. In terms of the United States, however, 1942 marked the mass arrival of US forces in Britain; the first successful bombing of Japan; the victorious Battle of Midway; the first Japanese land defeat at the Battle of Milne Bay; the retaking of Guadalcanal; and the earliest successes of the Manhattan Project (in the guise of the first self-sustaining nuclear chain reaction). At this stage it had become obvious to all enlightened observers that Britain, as a world power, while not yet having reached its absolute nadir, was definitely on the way down, whilst the United States was on the way up.

Summary

A follow-on to 10/100 – 1600 [The British Empire I], in which Nostradamus shows the British Empire both at its inception and at its zenith. By terming the British Empire a 'humane' one, he appears to be asking his readers to concentrate on the Empire's unifying, rather than on its colonising, aspects.

KING CHARLES I OF ENGLAND

Devant le peuple sang sera respandu

Que du haut ciel ne viendra esloigner:

Mais d'un long temps ne sera entendu

L'esprit d'un seul le viendra tesmoigner.

In front of the people blood will be spilled

It will not be far removed from the heavens

But for a long time no one will hear

The spirit of even one person bearing witness.

This is a truly extraordinary quatrain, and with an exact index date, which previous Nostradamian commentators have – somewhat inevitably – ignored. The index date is 49, and refers, of course, to 1649, the year in which King Charles I of England was beheaded on the orders of the 135 Commissioners of the House of Commons (Republicans and Parliamentarians to a man), of whom 59 signed the actual death warrant. We know it is a king we are dealing with here for Nostradamus speaks of the 'spilled blood' as being 'not far removed from the heavens'. Charles was a staunch (I use the word advisedly) believer in the divine right of kings, which stipulates that a monarch owes his rule directly to the Will of God, and that such monarchs are ordained – rather than merely raised – to the throne. Divine right also carried with it the concept of the 'mandate of heaven' (to which Nostradamus may be referring), and which harkens back to ancient China, and to the idea that heaven would respond in kind to a just and responsible ruler.

The last two lines are pretty much self-evident, as they describe the situation of collective silence (and collective guilt?) in Cromwell's England in the immediate aftermath of the execution, and which continued for a further nine years until the Lord Protector's death [*see* 1/53 – 1653: Oliver Cromwell]. Hearsay has it that a communal moan went up as the anonymous headsman's axe cleaved through the royal vertebrae, and that many members of the crowd surged forward to dip their kerchiefs in the royal blood, either as a protection against the king's evil (a.k.a. scrofula: *'le roy te touche, Dieu te guerisse'* – 'the king touches you, God cures you' – it is known, for instance, that Charles II, Charles's son, touched 92,107 persons in one year for similar reasons) or in a desire to bear witness to something that felt inherently (i.e. instinctively, as opposed to logically) wrong.

Summary

The monarchist Nostradamus would almost certainly have disapproved of the regicide and *lèse majesté* encapsulated by Charles I's execution – so the good news lies in the fact that moral restitution *was* eventually made, in the form of the Restoration of the Stuart monarchs in 1660.

BIRTH OF WILLIAM OF ORANGE

De l'aquatique triplicité naistra.

D'un qui fera le jeudi pour sa feste

Son bruit, loz, regne, sa puissance croistra,

Par terre et mer aux Oriens tempeste.

A triumvirate will arise from the water

One of whom will choose Thursday for his feast day

He will be both renowned and praised, and his reign and power will grow

The easterners will be battered by land and by sea.

The triumvirate/triplicity that Nostradamus mentions in line 1 may be taken both literally, in the sense of an alliance of three, and metaphorically, in the sense of a man, or men, under the dominance of the three great environmentally and emotionally sensitive water signs of Cancer (liquid/cardinal), Scorpio (solid/fixed), and Pisces (gas/mutable). This man will choose Thursday (or Thor's day) for his feast day, and the triplicity may therefore find itself echoed once again in the form of the old French proverb which goes: '*Cela arrivera la Semaine des trois jeudis*' – 'That will only ever happen when we get a week with three Thursdays in it'. Maundy Thursday, of course, is the day before Good Friday, and is considered particularly propitious, in that it was the day Jesus Christ was afforded a new mandate (John 13: 34), which commanded men and women to 'love one another'. This commandment then transposed itself in medieval times into a day in which maunds (i.e. baskets) of food were laid out and distributed for the poor.

With all this in mind we are left with a deeply charitable and emotionally sensitive leader of the West, with an index date of 50 – in this commentator's view, therefore, the quatrain refers to William III of Orange, who was born on the 14th November 1650 (a Scorpio, therefore) and instantly became Prince of the Dutch House of Orange, succeeding his father who had died only eight days earlier of smallpox. William was later to win the English, Scottish and Irish crowns as a result of the Glorious Revolution of 1688 [*see* 4/98 – 1688–89: The Glorious Revolution], and the largely benevolent and religiously tolerant – both the Act Of

Toleration and the Bill of Rights were passed under his aegis –
joint reign of William and his wife, Mary, and following
them, of their daughter Anne (the triumvirate), marked the
beginning of the true parliamentary period of British rule,
and eventually led to the successful unification of Great
Britain, as encapsulated within the 1707 Acts Of Union
[*see* 10/71 – 1707: The Unification Of Great Britain and 5/7 –
1707: The Acts Of Union].

Summary

A quatrain foretelling the birth of the man, William of
Orange, who was destined to act as the principle catalyst for
the unification of what was eventually to become the
Kingdom of Great Britain.

OLIVER CROMWELL

1653

1 / 53

Las qu'on verra grand peuple tourmenté

Et la loy saincte en totale ruine

Par autres loyx toute Chrestienté,

Quand d'or d'argent trouve nouvelle mine.

Alas that we should see a great nation in
torment

And Holy Law in total ruin

All Christianity will be governed by other laws

When from gold, silver will find a new face.

Alchemy, first of all – clearly delineated in line 4. For the ancient alchemists, gold represented the sun and silver the moon – here, however, Nostradamus is overturning the usual alchemical trend, by making silver out of gold, and not the reverse. This implies a philosophical downgrading, roughly akin to Chaucer's dictum 'But al thyng which that shineth as the gold/Nis nat gold, as that I have herd told;' (*Canterbury Tales*, The Canon's Yeoman's Tale, lines 962–3). Chaucer's dictum was itself adapted (as the author generously implies) from Alanus de Insulis's '*Non teneas aurum totum quod splendet ut aurum/Nec pulcrum pomum quodlibet esse bonum*' – from the *Parabolae*, a book which Nostradamus would also undoubtedly have read, for Alain de l'Isle (1128–1202) – *nom de plume* de Insulis – was a famous French theologian who had lived for some time in Montpellier, Nostradamus's university town (he is sometimes also known as Alanus de Montepesullano on that account). Chaucer goes even further along Nostradamus's contrarian route, in lines 1476–79 of the CYT: 'For whoso maketh God his adversarie,/As for to werken any thyng in contrarie/Of his wil, certes, never shal he thryve,/Thogh that he multiplie terme of his lyve.'

Now to the index date of 53, which leads us straight to 1653, the year in which Oliver Cromwell became Lord Protector of England, Scotland and Ireland (bearing out Thomas Hobbes's *Leviathan* predictions, written two years earlier). Cromwell's Puritan Protestantism would have been anathema to the Catholic Nostradamus, and he describes England's descent into fundamental Protestantism very well, suggesting that no good will come of it. He was right, of course, and the Providentialist Cromwell was to die only five years later, his legacy in ruins, to be replaced by a marginally less enlightened (if certainly more entertaining) Stuart pragmatism.

Summary

Nostradamus bemoans Puritanism and Providentialism as a byway off the strait track, and looks forward to a return to the so-called 'True Faith' of Catholicism. To that extent, at least, he would have considered the Cromwell interregnum a good thing, and its long-term effects benevolent.

THE GREAT FIRE OF LONDON

2 SEPTEMBER 1666

2 / 51

Le sang du juste à Londres sera faute
Bruslez par fouldres de vingt trois les six.
La dame antique cherra de place haute:
De mesme secte plusieurs seront occis.

The blood of the upright will be absent from London

She will burn up suddenly in the year '66

The old lady will fall from her high place

Many other Protestant churches will be destroyed, too.

It might at first glance seem odd to declare a quatrain accurately foretelling the Great Fire of London as good news, but that, in many ways, is what it was. Look at it this way: the fire killed only six people, when the death count could have been in the thousands; it paved the way for the reconstruction of London by Christopher Wren, including the building and consecration of forty-nine new churches, and his masterpiece, the new St Paul's; it virtually eradicated the plague, which had killed 17,440 people (from a population of 93,000) the previous year; it got rid of a significant number of unsanitary medieval slums; and the lessons learned from it, in the form of building (most pre-Great Fire houses were half-timbered, covered with pitch and tar, and had thatched roofs), firefighting, and emergency clearance, ensured that London would never again be threatened with total destruction, whatever the cause.

Now to the quatrain, which must stand as one of Nostradamus's greatest and most successfully realised. The 'blood of the upright' may be taken to refer sardonically to the nobility, many of whom were quick to leave London – the king, of course, famously only learned of the full extent of the fire from Samuel Pepys's eyewitness account, brought to him in the comparative safety of Whitehall (although that, too, was threatened on the final day of the fire). Four fifths of the city was destroyed in the fire (13,200 houses, 50 livery halls, 87 churches, covering, in total, an area of 436 acres), which Nostradamus dates with total accuracy by multiplying 20 by 3 plus 6 = 66. The 'old lady' in line 3 is St Paul's Cathedral, which was destroyed alongside 86 more of the city's 109 churches (*secte*, in line 4, is the Catholic Nostradamus's way of telling us that these are protestant churches going up in flames, for to the Catholic Church in Nostradamus's time, the Protestant Church was, most definitely, a sect). And to cap it all, the second line may also be read, if taken euphonically (*see* Introduction), as '*brulez par foudre divin, troyes, les six*' ('burned by divine lightning, like Troy, but only six died'). Only six people did die in the fire.

Poet Laureate John Dryden wrote the following, in his epic poem about 1666, entitled *Annus Mirabilis* [*see* 2/66 – 1666: Sir Isaac Newton's *Annus Mirabilis*]:

> Methinks already from this chemic flame,
> I see a city of more precious mould:
> Rich as the town which gives the Indies name,
> With silver paved, and all divine with gold.

Summary

It may seem odd to term a quatrain that predicts a terrible fire as 'good news', but the long-term effects of the Great Fire of London included an end to the plague, the Wren reconstruction, and the inception of insurance and, as a direct consequence, effective firefighting services. It was a transformational event, therefore, and fully deserves its 'good news' status.

SIR ISAAC NEWTON'S
ANNUS MIRABILIS

1666

2 / 66

Par grans dangiers le captif eschapé,
Peu de temps grand la fortune changée:
Dans le palais le peuple est attrapé,
Par bon augure la cité est assiegée.

In a time of great danger, the captive escapes

Very soon the fortunes of the great man change

The people are trapped inside the palace

By a miracle the city is besieged.

The year 1666 was generally considered to be Sir Isaac Newton's *annus mirabilis*, rather as 1905 was to be that of his distinguished successor, Albert Einstein [*see* 3/5 – 1905: Albert Einstein's *Annus Mirabilis*]. Despite his eccentricities, prejudices and foibles, Newton was undoubtedly one of the most gifted scientists and mathematicians that has ever lived, and the normally overused word 'genius' may reasonably be used to describe him – in mathematical physicist Joseph Louis Lagrange's words, 'Newton was the greatest genius that ever existed and the most fortunate, for we cannot find more than once a system of the world to establish.' Poet Laureate John Dryden (also a scion of Newton's alma mater, Trinity College) so firmly believed that 1666 was a unique year, that he coined the words *annus mirabilis* ('the year of miracles'), and used them as the title of his poem about the period, which viewed the year of Nostradamus's index date as crucial to the future of mankind:

> This I foretell from your auspicious care,
> Who great in search of God and nature grow;
> Who best your wise Creator's praise declare,
> Since best to praise his works is best to know.
>
> O truly royal! who behold the law
> And rule of beings in your Maker's mind:
> And thence, like limbecks, rich ideas draw,
> To fit the levell'd use of human-kind.

(Note: Limbecks/alembics were flasks used by alchemists to distil or purify liquids)

It was at this crucial period of transition into the modern world that Newton, together with his fellow students, found himself unexpectedly dismissed from Trinity College, Cambridge, on account of the plague ('in a time of great danger, the captive escapes'). The unexpected lacunae of 1665 and 1666 were to prove particularly productive for Newton, and directly produced the 'change of fortune' referred to in line 2, for in the following year, thanks to his groundbreaking early studies, Newton was elected a fellow of the college (1st October 1667), probably filling the vacancy caused by Abraham Cowley's unexpected death the previous summer. During this enforced period of intensive study at home (rather than under the guidance of his masters at college), Newton began those studies in calculus, optics, fluxions, pure mathematics, and the laws of gravity, that were to lay the foundations for his exponential success ten years later.

Both the final lines apply to Cambridge, and to the plague, and echo, to a certain extent, in their concept of 'good news' coming out of bad, both Dryden's 'year of wonders' poem and Nostradamus's parallel quatrains of 2/51 – 1666 [The Great Fire Of London], and 3/70 – 1770 [Virgilian Comfort Following The Great British Floods].

Summary

Newton is unexpectedly confined in Lincolnshire during a series of plague outbreaks, during which the earliest inception of his world-changing gravitational theory is triggered.

ANTONIO STRADIVARI

Aupres du jeune le vieux ange baisser
Et le viendra surmonter à la fin:
Dix ans esgaux au plus vieux rabaisser;
De trois d'eux l'un huitiesme seraphin.

The old angel bows before the younger one

But he will rise above him in the end

He is reduced to ten years of equality with the
old one

Of the three of them, only one becomes the
eighth seraphim.

The seraphim are angels of light, and they reside directly in the presence of God. Each has six wings and four heads – one for each of the cardinal directions – and they may not be seen by human eyes. Their upper wings are used for flying, their middle wings cover their eyes, and their lower wings cover their feet (or, according to some authorities, their genitalia). The seraphim are musical (they form part of the angelic choir, which constitutes the highest order in the hierarchy of angels), and one of their main duties is to sing the praises of the Lord (the Sanctus, or Trisagion), which they do using the words: 'Holy, holy, holy, is the Lord of hosts: the whole earth is full of his glory.' (Isaiah 6: 3 and Revelations 4: 8.)

This musical element is therefore crucial in any reading of this complex quatrain, and, following the musical link, we duly find that the index date of 69 leads us to 1669, the year in which Antonio Stradivari (1644-1737), 'touched by the hand of God', made his very first violin. Stradivari, then, is the 'old angel', and Bartolomeo Guiseppe Guarneri Del Gesù (1698–1744), his main rival, is the 'younger one'. The 'old one' in line 3 is Nicolò Amati (1596-1684), who, at least according to his own contemporaries, was by far the greater violin maker, and was both Stradivari's teacher, and that of Guarneri's grandfather, Andrea. Modern tastes prefer Stradivari, however, with Joseph Guarneri either sharing joint first place, or coming in a close second. Nostradamus's image of Stradivari becoming the eighth seraphim is a rather beautiful one, therefore, and no doubt reflects the master's ability to encapsulate light (*saraph* means 'to burn') in the making of his musical instruments, of which there were about 1,100 in all, including violins, violas, cellos, harps and guitars – of which perhaps 650 still survive in playable condition to this day.

Summary

A rather beautiful quatrain detailing the three greatest makers of violins, all of whom were said to have been 'touched by the very hand of God'. The greatest of 'good news', surely, given the unifying and healing capacity of great music.

GREEK SETTLERS FIND A HAVEN IN CORSICA

De l'Ambraxie et du pays de Thrace,
Peuple par mer mal et secours Gaulois,
Perpetuelle en Provence la trace,
Avec vestiges de leur coustume et loix.

From Ambracia and from Thrace

People sickened by the sea seek help from France

Traces of them remain in Provence

Together with vestiges of their customs and laws.

Ambracia, a province of ancient Corinthia, and founded between the years 650 and 625 BC by Gorgus, son of the tyrant Cypselus, is situated roughly seven miles from the Ambracian Gulf (near the modern-day Greek city of Arta). It, like Thrace (which now incorporates parts of Turkey, Bulgaria and Greece), was much involved in the Peloponnesian War (read Thucydides for further details), with both areas being conquered, at one time or another, by the near ubiquitous Philip II of Macedon (the father of Alexander the Great). The Aegean Sea lies almost exactly between the two areas Nostradamus mentions, and one therefore presumes that it must be the sea mentioned in line 2 – either that, or possibly the Mediterranean, for Provence (Nostradamus's birthplace) became part of Greece too, some twenty-five years after the founding of Ambracia, with Marseilles acting as the focus for intra-Mediterranean trade between the Greeks, the Phoenicians, the Ligurians, and, much later, circa 200 BC, the Romans.

So what is Nostradamus trying to do here? Is he simply showing nostalgia for Greek culture? Or is he retelling historical fact? The index date of 75 doesn't tell us much, although there may be some link with the long-standing Greek community of Cargèse, in Corsica, which is renowned for having two churches built directly opposite each other – a Latin Catholic church for the French, and an Orthodox church for the Greeks. This all occurred in 1675, which is fine as far as the index dating is concerned, for it also ties in with the 'people sickened by the sea' aspect of the quatrain, for a certain Captain Daniel had agreed to take

800 Greeks on the first tranche of their journey from Ottoman Greece to Corsica, and, during the course of the voyage, some 120 of the 800 emigrants died. Later on, when the French took Corsica from the Genoese, the Greeks refused to turn against their original Genoese benefactors, and it was only during the French Revolution that the Greeks and the French allied themselves together against the Jacobins from Vico. To this day the ritual used in the Greek Cargèse church is the Ancient Greek one of Athens and Constantinople, and exactly equivalent to that used in Marseilles.

Summary

In 1675, harassed by the Ottoman Turks, 800 Greeks seek succour from the Genoese, and are accorded a foothold in Corsica, which they maintain to this day under the French. The influx benefitted both sides, and led to numerous creative synergies.

THE GLORIOUS REVOLUTION

1688–89

4/89

Trente de Londres secret conjureront,

Contre leur Roi sur le pont l'entreprise:

Lui, fatalistes la mort degousteront,

Un Roi esleu blonde, natif de Frize.

Thirty Londoners will conspire in secret

Against their king; this to be undertaken by sea

He, and various fatalists, are disgusted by death

A blond king is elected, who was born in Friesland.

Anyone doubting Nostradamus's uncanny historical prescience has only to look at this quatrain, first published in 1557, and dealing, in detail, with events occurring over 130 years later; and also his two other quatrains of a similar ilk, namely 1/50 – 1650 [Birth Of William Of Orange], and 10/4 – 1704 [The Battle Of Blenheim]. All three are pinpoint accurate in their index dates, and deal with interlinked events that could not possibly have been construed or prognosticated in any way, means, or form, before their actual occurrence.

The 'blond king born in Friesland' is the Saxon William of Orange, who was formally invited by twenty-nine signatories – and the tacit agreement of the Duke of Marlborough to bring his troops over, at dead of night, from James II's faction to that of William – to sail up the Thames with his fleet and take over the English throne in the name of his wife Mary (James II's daughter) and his mother Mary Stuart (eldest daughter of Charles I). James II and his commander-in-chief, John Churchill (later 1st Duke of Marlborough) are the 'fatalists, disgusted by death' in line 3, and it was James's decision to run rather than to fight, and John Churchill's decision to mutiny rather than to serve an unpopular king, that made of the Glorious Revolution of 1688 a bloodless one, also.

SUMMARY

One of Nostradamus's finest quatrains, detailing the plot by members of James II's court to invite William of Orange to take over and secure Protestant England.

RECONSTITUTION

Cydron, Raguse, la cité au sainct Hieron,
Reverdira le medicant succours,
Mort fils de Roy par mort de deux heron,
L'Arabe Ongrie feront un mesme cours:

Cedron, Ragusa, and the city of Saint Heron

Will grow green again with medical help

The king's son will die because of the death
of two herons

Arabia and Hungary will flow in a similar
direction.

Cedron (meaning the black torrent) was, according to the biblical John 18: 1, the brook that flowed through the ravine below the eastern wall of Jerusalem, a city which was itself destroyed by the Romans in the year 70. Ragusa Ibla is an ancient town in Sicily (originally called Hybla Heraea), situated about an hour's drive from the city of Syracuse, and notable for its near total destruction in the infamous earthquake of 1693, in which more than 5,000 people were said to have lost their lives. The city of Heron might possibly be construed as Alexandria, if one takes Heron as being Heron of Alexandria (10 BC–75 BC), one of the most important Greek mathematicians of his time, specialising in geometry and mechanics, and the inventor of both a steam turbine and a formula for the area of a triangle. Interestingly, the 'Saint' aspect of Heron might also refer to another native of Alexandria, namely St Heron, whose feast day falls on the 14th December, and who ended up being burned at the stake in one of the city squares during Emperor Septimius Severus's persecution of 202.

The city of Alexandria – including its famous library, which had previously suffered inadvertent partial destruction under Julius Caesar in 48 BC, and advertent destruction under Aurelian in the third century, and again during the Christian riots of 391, following the decree of Theophilus – was of course famously destroyed once and for all by Omar, Caliph of Baghdad, in 642, and its books used to heat the city's water supply (thus the 'Arabian' connection). In addition to this, when taken euphonically, line 4 also gives us *L'Arabe en gris* (the grey Arab), which may be construed as pointing to the Shatt El Arab river, a continuation of the Tigris (which runs straight through Omar's Baghdad), and which is so full of natural silt that it is sometimes called the 'grey river'. So as well as the rivers, we are left with three cities which have at some time or another in their history suffered almost total destruction by outside forces, and a king's son who will die because of the death of two herons.

The water imagery would appear to be paramount here, and to afford us the most clues towards a reading of the quatrain, as it is echoed in every line: the black torrent in line 1; the greening, presumably by water, in line 2; the two herons in line 3; and the word *cours*, in line 4, which generally describes the flow or current of a river. In ancient bestiaries (such as the Aberdeen, Folio 53 V), the heron was known for its fear of rain and for its capacity to fly over the clouds in avoidance of storms – but it was also called after Tantalus, the king who betrayed the secrets of the gods. Tantalus's betrayal consisted of the murder and dismemberment of his own son ('the king's son'), Pelops, whose disguised body Tantalus then served up to the gods during a feast. When they discovered the trick, the gods immersed Tantalus up to his neck in water, with the diabolical condition that when he bent down to drink, all the water drained away before he could manage to touch it with his lips (thus the origin of the word 'tantalised'). They also gave Pelops back his life, reconstituting the arm that had been partially eaten by Demeter, with ivory. And thus my title for the quatrain, 'Reconstitution'.

SUMMARY

It seems as if Nostradamus is dredging up famous examples of disasters from the past in order to demonstrate to people in the future that, though things may seem grim at the time of whatever calamity has befallen them, all is not necessarily lost – that gold, in other words, might eventually be made from silver, just as the alchemists suggested.

JOHANN SEBASTIAN BACH

Devant moustier trouvé enfant besson,

D'heroic sang de moine et vestutisque:

Son bruit par secte langue et puissance son

Qu'on dira fort eleué le vopisque.

The son of a twin will be found in front of a monastery

Fruit of the heroic blood of a monk, and of ancient lineage

His fame will be known through Protestantism, tongue, and powerful sound

So that one might say that the survivor of this twin will indeed be raised high.

The Bach family was of ancient Hungarian origin, and were so numerous, and of such high standing in the Thuringian community – to which they came after their ejection from Hungary by the Hapsburgs on account of their adherence to Lutheranism (the 'sect' in line 3) – that around Erfurt and Eisenach any musician eventually came to be known as a 'Bach', whether he was actually related to the family or not. The Bachs went on to produce seven generations of musicians, spanning in time from the age of Luther (who studied at the University of Erfurt, and became, famously, a 'monk' at the Augustinian Erfurt Monastery), to that of Bismarck.

The key to this quatrain, lies in the concept of a twin, and in the index date of 95. Put the two together, and one gets 1695, which is the year in which Bach's father, Johann Ambrosius, unexpectedly died, a bare two years after his twin brother Johann Christoph, and less than a year after Bach's mother, Elisabeth Lämerhirt, who had predeceased him. During his lifetime, Bach became the musical conscience of German Protestantism, and this link between Martin Luther (the 'monk' and the 'monastery') and Bach (the 'son of a twin' and the 'fomenter of a powerful sound'), makes of this quatrain – which has never before been interpreted in this way – something of a triumph.

SUMMARY

A quatrain detailing both the religious affiliation and the musical legacy of possibly the greatest composer of them all, Johann Sebastian Bach.

POPE INNOCENT XII

QUATRAIN

8/99

Par la puissance des trois rois temporelz,

En autre lieu sera mis le saint siege:

Où la substance de l'esprit corporel,

Sera remys et receu pour vrai siège.

By the power of three temporal kings

The papal seat will be moved

Whence the substance of the physical spirit

Will be surrendered, and received in the true seat.

The index date of 99 is the key here, for it points to 1699, and the emendation of the Second Partition Treaty between Louis XIV of France and William III of England, dividing Charles II's Spanish kingdom between Archduke Charles of Austria (Spain, the Spanish Netherlands and Spanish America), Dauphin Louis of France (Naples, the Lorraine and Sicily), and Charles, Duke of Lorraine (Milan). This rather high-handed carve-up led directly to the 1701 War of the Spanish Succession.

The year 1699 also saw the anti-nepotistic and anti-simoniacal Pope Innocent XII's Apostolic Constitution condemning Archbishop François Fénelon's *Explanation On The Maxims Of The Saints On The Interior Life* (*Explication Des Maximes Des Saints Sur La Vie Intérieure*), twenty-three of whose propositions were excoriated as 'temerarious, scandalous, ill-sounding, offensive to pious ears, pernicious in practice, and even erroneous' at the express behest of Jacques-Bénigne Bossuet, who advocated a differing (and yet equally tendentious) form of expression for the love of God from that of the anti-monarchical Fénelon. This Pignatelli pope became, not uncoincidentally, the true moral hero of Robert Browning's *The Ring And The Book*, an extended poem of 21,000 lines in which Browning describes the pope (who was to die the very next year) as 'one of well-nigh decayed intelligence'. Browning goes on to show, however, in Pope Innocent's rejection of Count Franceschini's appeal against the death penalty for the unjust murder of his wife, that morality must always triumph over expedience (that good must always triumph over evil, in other words) – something that was to be doubly struck home in the long-term European and North American fallout from the fiasco of the Second Partition Treaty, which did, indeed, 'move' the papal seat.

Summary

Nostradamus uses the index date of 99 to show us a number of moral examples, in each of which political or religious expedience eventually gives way to moral clarity – with the moral court of the battlefield considered inferior to that of the intellect, in the guise of Pope Innocent XII.

BRITISH NAVAL VICTORY AT VIGO

23 OCTOBER 1702

10/2

Voille gallere voil de nef cachera,
La grande classe viendra sortir la moindre
Dix naves proches le tourneront poulser,
Grande vaincue unis à foy joindre.

The sails of the galleys will hide those of the
smaller boats

The great fleet will bring out the lesser one

Ten nearby boats will force it back

The great allies, united in faith, are vanquished.

It is at least arguable that the effective use of Britain's ever-burgeoning navy during the War Of The Spanish Succession (1701–14) – a war nominally between Britain and its allies, Austria and The Netherlands, versus France (with Spain along for the ride) – laid the groundwork for Britain's domination of the seas for the next two centuries. Given Nostradamus's index date of 2, it would seem that this quatrain describes the first great British naval victory of the war, at Vigo, in 1702. This battle took place much as described in the quatrain, and consisted of a combined Anglo-Dutch fleet, under the command of Admiral Sir George Rooke (the 'great fleet'), coming to terms with a Franco-Spanish fleet of thirty ships, whose job it was to protect the annual Spanish treasure fleet fresh out of Cuba (the 'lesser'). A further clue, and proof that the victory at Vigo is indeed the subject of this quatrain, comes in line 3, with 'ten nearby boats will force it back' – the British had exactly ten fire ships, whose job it was to blockade the French ships within Vigo harbour, and to prevent them from bringing their heavy guns to bear on the interlopers.

The battle was an unmitigated disaster for the French, and a complete victory for Admiral Rooke and his allies – the Vigo forts were taken and the entirety of the French/Spanish fleet either burned, secured, or forced aground. The bulk of the Spanish treasure, though, proved to have been previously transhipped, and so Rooke had to content himself with a mere 14,000 pounds' worth of bullion, and a death tally of 2,000 enemy sailors to 800 British and Dutch killed. The battle, however, was instrumental in giving the British the beginnings of their later Mediterranean supremacy, cemented by the destruction of the French fleet at Toulon in 1707.

Summary

The 'great allies, united in faith' are the French and Spanish Catholics, and they are vanquished at the Battle of Vigo by the Protestant British, alongside their equally Protestant allies, the Dutch, marking the beginning of Britain's near two-and-a-half-century domination of the seas.

THE BATTLE OF BLENHEIM

13 AUGUST 1704

10/4

Sus la minuict conducteur de l'armee

Se saulvera, subit esvanouy,

Sept ans apres la fame non blasmee,

A son retour ne dira oncq ouy.

At the stroke of midnight the army commander

Will save himself, vanishing suddenly

Seven years later, his fame still unblemished

They will be all for his return.

John Churchill, 1st Duke of Marlborough (1650–1722), as well as being possibly the most consummate military genius that England has ever produced, was also a canny political mover and shaker (nobly aided in this respect by his wife, Sarah Jennings). A staunch Anglican, he began to turn against his former master James II following the abrupt arrogation of his command to Louis de Duras, Earl of Feversham, during the Monmouth Rebellion of 1685. Already a friend of William of Orange, Marlborough later deserted in the dead of night ('at the stroke of midnight') to his cause during the so-called Glorious Revolution of 1688 [see 1/50 – 1650: Birth Of William Of Orange and 4/89 – 1688–89: The Glorious Revolution], thus 'saving himself' and ensuring the continuation and fruition of what was to become a stupendous military career.

Following his public disgrace, when it was discovered that he had been secretly communicating with James II and the French (in May 1694 he had apparently disclosed to James the English plan to invade the town of Brest), Churchill 'vanished' to Canada to pursue his interests in the Hudson's Bay Company, of which he had briefly been governor. Exactly 'seven years later' he was recalled by William in the run-up to the War Of The Spanish Succession (1701–14), which he fought, following William's death, largely under the aegis of Queen Anne (James II's daughter), whose favourite attendant his wife was.

The Duke of Marlborough's greatest battle, and that which cemented his reputation and provided the name for the estate granted to him by a grateful queen and nation, was the Battle of Blenheim, on the 13th August 1704, in which he defeated Marshal Tallard's superior-strength army through the use of enlightened feint, resulting in more than 30,000 French and Bavarians killed or wounded, with 11,000 French surrendering. Marlborough became the toast of England, with even the likes of Joseph Addison writing him encomiums, in the form of *A Campaign, A Poem, To His Grace The Duke Of Marlborough*:

> So when an angel by divine command
> With rising tempests shaks a guilty land,
> Such as of late o'er pale Britannia past,
>
> Calm and serene he drives the furious blast;
> And, pleas'd th' Almighty's orders to perform,
> Rides in the whirlwind, and directs the storm.

Summary

A masterly quatrain delineating the early chequered career of John Churchill, 1st Duke of Marlborough, and its later apotheosis thanks to his signal victory at the Battle of Blenheim.

THE BATTLE OF TURIN

Au roy l'agure sus le chef la main mettre,

Viendra prier pour la paix Italique:

A la main gauche viendra changer le sceptre,

De Roy viendra Empereur pacifique.

Both the augur and the chief will lay their hands
upon the King

He will come to plead for peace with Italy

The sceptre will change to the left hand

From the King will come a peaceful Emperor.

Given this quatrain's index date of 6, one is at first tempted by the story of Napoleon making his brother, Louis I Napoleon Bonaparte, king of Holland in 1806. Although he didn't last very long (his brother forced him to abdicate in 1810 on the pretext that he was too pro-Dutch), Koning Lodewijk I was seemingly a good king – his nickname was Louis the Good – and he has the added advantage that his third son, Charles Louis Napoleon Bonaparte, later became Emperor Napoleon III of France. The Italian connection is harder to find, although Louis did have an illegitimate son, François de Castelvecchio.

On balance, though, the quatrain is far more likely to refer to the Battle of Turin, fought on the 7th September 1706 as part of the War of the Spanish Succession, and which resulted in a decisive victory for the allied forces, under the leadership of Victor Amadeus II, later king of Sicily – and after that, thanks to a swap, of Sardinia ('the sceptre will change to the left hand') – together with the famously celibate Prince Eugene of Savoy. The battle resulted in the complete removal of French troops from northern Italy in 1707. Victor Amadeus II, through his daughter, Marie Adelaide, was also the grandfather of Louis XV of France, and great-great-grandfather of Louis XVIII and Charles X.

SUMMARY

The Battle of Turin, resulted in the complete withdrawal of French troops from Italy – the larger War of the Spanish Succession, under whose aegis the battle was fought, was to last from 1701, to the 1713–14 treaties of Utrecht and Rastatt.

THE UNIFICATION OF GREAT BRITAIN

1707

10/71

La terre et l'air gelleront si grand eau

Lors qu'on viendra pour jeudi venerer,

Ce qui sera jamais ne feut si beau,

Des quatre pars le viendront honnorer.

The earth and the air will freeze such an expanse
of water

When Thursday becomes revered

That the future will be more beautiful than ever

Receiving homage from the four corners
of the world.

Many commentators have contrived an association with US Thanksgiving Day for this quatrain, as Thanksgiving traditionally falls on the fourth Thursday of November, but, to this commentator at least, the idea smacks a little of tendentiousness. Nostradamus is far more likely to have had in mind the Thursday of the Last Supper, in which Jesus washed his disciples' feet before passing on to them his '*mandatum novum do vobis ut diligatis invicem sicut dilexi vos*' edict, which, translated, means 'a new commandment I give unto you, that you love one another as I have loved you' (John 13: 34). This would link the quatrain back to quatrain number 1/50 – 1650 [Birth Of William Of Orange], and in particular to line 2, which reads 'One of whom will choose Thursday for his feast day'.

If that were to be the case, then the quatrain could be construed as a description of the British Empire ('receiving homage from the four corners of the world'), whose origins lay in the gradual unification of Great Britian which occurred under the triumvirate of William III and Mary, and their daughter Anne, and coalesced inside the Acts Of Union of 1707. [*See* 5/7 – 1707 The Acts Of Union]

SUMMARY

A description of the early steps leading to the eventual creation of the British Empire – a generally benevolent, trading-based empire which encapsulated, at its zenith, all four corners of the globe.

THE ACTS OF UNION

Du Triumvir seront trouvez les os,

Cherchant profond tresor aenigmatique,

Ceux d'alentour ne seront en repos

De concaver marbre et plomb metalique.

The bones of the Triumvirate will be found

During the search for a profound and
enigmatic treasure

Those around about will not rest

In the hollowing out of marble and
metallic lead.

The index date of 7 gives us our clue here, for it points up the year 1707, in which the Acts of Union were passed, formalising the unification of the 'triumvirate' of England, Scotland, and, by previous default, Wales, into one United Kingdom of Great Britain, under one all-powerful Parliament. There had been three previous attempts to unite Great Britain (in 1606, 1667 and 1689), but these had all failed, and 1707 was to prove the crucial year in the hastening process, securing, as it did, the formal future of the Church of Scotland ('a profound and enigmatic treasure') as final arbiter in ecclesiastical matters north of the border, being both established and free at same time. The final line may be taken as symptomatic of the numerous protests held against the union, and which resulted in both death by bullet ('metallic lead'), and the formal burial and memorialising ('the hollowing out of marble') during the radical uprisings of the late eighteenth and early nineteenth centuries.

SUMMARY

The passing of the formal Acts Of Union which created the United Kingdom of Great Britain in 1707, and, despite strong resistance from supranational independence parties, still maintains its hold to this day.

THE SONG OF LA PALISSE

En la frontiere de Caussade et Charlus,
Non guieres loing du fonds de la vallee,
De ville franche musicque à son de luths,
Environnez combouls et grand myttee.

On the border between Caussade and Charlus

Not very far from the valley estate

Lute music will sound from the free city
(Villefranche)

Incorporating cymbals and a famous myth.

Jacques II de Chabannes, Lord of la Palice, Chevalier, Baron de Curton et de Rochefort, Seigneur de Caussade (*see* quatrain), Madic, Charlus (*see* quatrain), la Dailhe, Aurires, Solon-la-Gane, Saignes, la Roche-Machalin et Tinires, was made Grand Master of France in 1511, and later Marshall, under François I. La Palice was known for his valour, and for his desire always to be at the forefront in any combat. Despite being taken prisoner for a second time at Guinegate in 1513, he escaped, and took part in the capture of Villefranche (*see* quatrain) and in the battle of Marignan. He was killed, in 1525, at the famous Battle of Pavia, considered by many to be the first great modern battle, and in which canoneers replaced knights for the first time, resulting in the virtual annihilation of the standing French army. And that, in normal circumstances, would have been that.

But one curious thing emerges from the fog of battle, and it relates rather nicely to Nostradamus's otherwise elusive quatrain – La Palice's soldiers composed a song about him. The song, in its original form, went: '*Hélas, s'il n'était pas mort, il ferait encore envie*' – 'Alas, if he wasn't dead, they would still be envying him'. Now in Old French (and as with Nostradamus), esses and effs may sometimes be printed or written to look exactly like one another – most times, when this happens, the meaning is obvious from the context, but in the case of La Palice's song, serendipity has it that were the ess to be mistaken for the eff, it would create a meaning so sublime in its tautological illogic that it was inevitable that, somewhere along the line, a poet with a humorous streak should pick it up and run with it.

The poet in question was Bernard de la Monnoye (1641–1728), and he read the original French as '*Hélas, s'il n'était pas mort, il serait encore en vie*' – 'Alas, if he wasn't dead, he would still be alive.' Galvanised by this happy occurrence, de la Monnoye set to work. First, he coined the neologism '*lapalissade*', meaning an utterly obvious truth, or truism. Not content with this achievement, however, the French Academician went on to write a truly catchy song to cement his discovery, which he entitled the *Chanson De La Palisse*. Here's a taster:

Monsieur d'la Palisse est mort,	Monsieur de la Palice is dead,
il est mort devant Pavie,	He died before Pavie,
Un quart d'heure avant sa mort	A quarter of an hour earlier
il était encore en vie	He was still alive
Il fut par un triste sort	By a sad twist of fate
blessé d'une main cruelle,	He was wounded by a cruel hand,
On croit, puisqu'il en est mort,	One assumes (because he died of it)
que la plaie était mortelle.	That the wound was mortal.
Regretté de ses soldats,	Lamented by his men,
il mourut digne d'envie,	He died an enviable death,
Et le jour de son trépas	The day he died
fut le dernier de sa vie	Was his last

Il mourut le vendredi,	His death occurred on a Friday,
le dernier jour de son âge,	The last day he would age,
S'il fût mort le samedi,	If it had been a Saturday,
il eût vécu davantage.	He would have lived even longer.

Summary

An utterly delightful quatrain in which Nostradamus teases out an as yet nonexistent myth concerning a man with whose military exploits and glorious death he would no doubt have been achingly familiar.

KING PHILIP V OF SPAIN

L'un des plus grands fuira aux Espaignes

Qu'en longue playe apres viendra saigner

Passant copies par les hautes montaignes

Devastant tout et puis en paix regner.

One of the great will hurry off to Spain

Which will suffer from much bloodletting and scarification

Armies will cross the high mountain passes

Devastating everything – later he will reign in peace.

In the course of reading this quatrain in the original French, all one's instincts tell one that it simply must relate to Philip V of Spain, who was also known as the 'king who ruled twice'. A manic depressive, prone to fits of melancholy (possibly inherited from his Bavarian Wittelsbach ancestors, who were considered to possess a madness gene), he also inherited the priapism of his Bourbon ancestors, something which contributed to his almost complete subsumation in the bodily functions of his first wife, Marie Louise of Savoy (culminating in Philip's having to be levered off her body on her deathbed – he missed her funeral, however, as he was out hunting). This was followed by domination by his second wife, Elizabeth Farnese, largely on the grounds of the withholding and then granting of her sexual favours in exchange for power (Philip was inordinately holy, and categorically refused to consider taking a mistress).

In the first part of his reign the French-born Philip saw massive sections of the Spanish empire gobbled up, thanks to the War of the Spanish Succession, by a phalanx of greedy outsiders (mostly British and Austrian, it has to be said) – Minorca went, followed by Gibraltar, the Spanish Netherlands, Sardinia, Milan and Naples, together with Sicily and parts of the Milanese. Disgusted with himself, Philip abdicated in favour of his son Luis I, and retired to a monastery, only to return to the throne later that year when Luis unexpectedly died of smallpox ('later he will reign in peace'). Struck down by melancholia once again, Philip constructed an extraordinary regimen for himself during which he existed largely at night – he later claimed that he had been healed by the great castrato singer, Carlo Broschi Farinelli, who was somehow persuaded to sing the exact same four arias to the king and his ever-present queen, every night for twenty years.

In the final equation, however, Philip must be deemed rather a success, in that he secured the throne of Spain for the Bourbons, and was prevented (innumerable times apparently) from further impulsive abdications, until he succumbed, quite naturally, to a cerebral haemorrhage, ceding the throne to his son, Ferdinand VI (another melancholic – Ferdinand died of grief after the death of his beloved wife, Maria Barbara, in 1759).

Summary

Good news for the Bourbons, whose rights to the throne of Spain were secured (seemingly in perpetuity) by the two tempestuously dotty kings mentioned in the commentary to this quatrain.

BONNIE PRINCE CHARLIE

16 APRIL 1746

6/46

Un juste sera en exile renvoyé,

Par pestilence aux confins de Nonseggle:

Response au rouge le fera desvoyé,

Roi retirant à la Rane et à l'aigle.

An upright man will be sent back into exile

Through corruption, to the remote area of
Nonseggle

His reply to the red one will send him out of
sight

The king withdrawing to the Frog and the Eagle.

The Jacobite defeat at Culloden Moor on the 16th April 1746 (*note* Nostradamus's exact index date of 46) was seriously good news for the Hanoverian English, and a disaster for the Highland Scots, destroying, as it did, all chances of restoring the Stuarts to the throne, and taking with it what remained of the old Highland way of life. The upright man in line 1 is, of course, Bonnie Prince Charlie, son of the Old Pretender, who raised his standard at Glenfinann, on the 19th August 1745, in a bid to oust George II and replace him with his father, James Edward Stuart, who would then have become James III (and VIII of Scotland). The 'red one' in line 3 is the just turned twenty-five-year-old William, Duke of Cumberland, leader of the redcoats, and also known as 'Butcher' or 'Bloody' Cumberland, and the victor of the last battle (to date) ever to be fought on British soil.

Following a tragically botched attempt to march to London – an ambition which ended ignominiously at a pub in Derby – the by now alcoholic Charles made a psychologically unwise return to Scotland. Less than four months later, 5,000 ravenously hungry and footsore Jacobites, having inexplicably chosen the bog at Culloden as their battleground, faced up to a well-founded and well-fed government force numbering at least 8,000, and which included artillery and mounted dragoons. The outcome of the battle was pretty much of a foregone conclusion, therefore, and within an hour the Jacobites had been routed, and Cumberland had engendered a vindictive bloodbath which refused to discriminate between innocent bystanders, fleeing rebels, and inadvertent witnesses to the fiasco.

Thus began Bonnie Prince Charlie's famous five-month escapade, in which, with a £30,000 bounty on his head, he evaded all the forces set on his capture. With the help of the redoubtable Flora Macdonald, he succeeded in escaping from Skye clad in female attire, and, two months later, in boarding a cutter bound for France (both the 'frog' and the 'eagle' are explicit French emblems, the one of Paris, the other of the empire). His drinking, and, later on, his shabby mistreatment of his wife, caught up with him, however, and eventually led to his expedient repudiation by France and his death without male progeny – 'Nonseggle', in such a context, might conceivably refer to the literal and metaphorical nomansland into which Charles was exiled following the October 1748 treaty of Aix-La-Chapelle.

Summary

Good news for the English and a disaster for Scotland might be a fair summing up of the career of Bonnie Prince Charlie, the flawed leader of the Jacobite/Stuart cause, which culminated in the catastrophic defeat at the Battle of Culloden.

VIRGILIAN COMFORT FOLLOWING THE GREAT BRITISH FLOODS

1770

3/70

La grand Bretagne comprinse l'Angleterre,

Viendra par eaux si haut à inonder

La ligue neufue d'Ausonne fera guerre,

Que contre eux ils se viendront bander.

Great Britain, including England

Will be inundated by high floodwaters

The new league of Ausonia will fight back

Even though so many are united against them.

The year 1770 was a devastating one for Great Britain, at least as far as flooding was concerned, for watermarks dating from that time can be seen on the walls of Worcester Cathedral and on numerous other still-standing edifices, and the floods that hit Lynmouth on the 6th to 7th August of that year are now considered by many to be worse even than those of 1952. A contemporary chronicler has this to say about the tragedy:

> The river at Lynmouth by the late rain rose to
> such a degree as was never known by the
> memory of any man now living, which brought
> down great rocks of several tons each, and
> choked up the harbour. And also carried away
> the foundation under the Kay on that side of
> the river six foot down and ninety foot long, and
> some places two foot under the Kay, which
> stands now in great danger of falling.

Following hard on the heels of the August floods in southern England, the 18th October 1770 saw the Sussex rivers and water meadows completely flooded, and the great flood of the 17th November 1770 carried away the Shropshire half of the Teme Bridge, and, as if that weren't enough, there were also floods at Evesham and Tewkesbury (during which the town clerk famously circumnavigated the borough in a rowing boat).

Now to part two of the quatrain: Ausonia was the ancient name for Italy, assumed, by some commentators, to be taken from Auson, son of Ulysses, and father of the Ausones, and by others from the Greek word *Opikoi*, describing the early Italic Oscan-speaking people of southern Italy. The mention of a league, though, leads us directly to Virgil's *Aeneid*, Book XI, where, following the death of Aeneas's ally and protégé, Pallas, at the hands of Turnus, we read of Aeneas's almost filial mourning for his friend, and his anger at the humiliations Turnus had heaped upon his dead body. One can only assume that Nostradamus is making a tacit connection here between the humiliations nature contrives, and those of an arbitrary fate, and that he is asking us to take comfort from Aeneas's steadfast example:

> If, for my league against th' Ausonian state,
> Amidst their weapons I had found my fate,
> (Deserv'd from them,) then I had been return'd
> A breathless victor, and my son had mourn'd.
> Yet will I not my Trojan friend upbraid,
> Nor grudge th' alliance I so gladly made.
> 'T was not his fault, my Pallas fell so young,
> But my own crime, for having liv'd too long.

Summary

Nostradamus draws universal comfort from the human capacity to rise above natural vicissitudes, and to use them to enlightened advantage.

GEORGE WASHINGTON

15 JUNE 1775

5/75

Montera haut sur le bien plus à dextre,

Demourra assis sur la pierre quarree:

Vers le midi posé à la fenestre,

Baston tortu en main, bouche serree.

He will rise high over the one considerably to the
right of him

He will remain seated on the stone square

Towards the South, placed at the window

Crooked staff in hand, his mouth pursed.

Given the index date of 75 on this quatrain, it is most likely that it refers to the American War of Independence, and to the election of the then left-wing George Washington as commander-in-chief of the Continental Army, over the more conservative John Hancock – an event which took place on the 15th June 1775. John Adams was taking a calculated gamble in placing Washington, a southerner, over an army made up largely of northerners, but the gamble belatedly paid off (following Washington's shaky series of New York defeats in 1776) when he successfully led the main arm of the Continental Army across the Delaware River to destroy the Hessian conscript force at Trenton.

Washington went on to become the first president of the United States, refusing to serve for a third term, and retiring to his Virginia plantation in 1797. The image that Nostradamus portrays of Washington 'seated on the stone square' may reasonably be taken to refer either to the famous statue of Washington seated on his horse, dated 1865, and the oldest in the New York City Parks collection, or to the roughly similar equestrian statue in the Boston Public Garden.

It would be nice to think that the 'crooked staff' in line 4 referred to the famous Crooked Billet Inn at Hatboro, in which George Washington was known to have held a series of important staff meetings in 1777 (honest!), but it is more likely to refer to the crooked knobbly cane given to Washington by Benjamin Franklin, and which is held to this day in the Smithsonian Institution. Franklin described the cane as follows: 'My fine crab-tree walking stick, with a gold head curiously wrought in the form of the cap of liberty, I give to my friend, and the friend of mankind, General Washington. If it were a Sceptre, he has merited it, and would become it.'

Summary

A beautiful quatrain, with an exact index dating, depicting the rise of George Washington, and his subsequent career as one of the United States' greatest presidents.

THE DECLARATION OF INDEPENDENCE

1776

1 / 76

D'un nom farouche tel proferé sera,

Que les trois seurs aurant fato le nom:

Puis grand peuple par langue et faict duira (dira)

Plus que nul autre aura bruit et renom.

His given name may seem a savage one

But both name and destiny were predicted by the three sisters

Following which a great people, through faith and language, will endure

His fame and his renown will surpass all others.

The 'savage name' is that of Englishman Thomas Paine, born to impoverished parents in Thetford, Norfolk, and later to become the intellectual progenitor of the American Revolution through his publication, in 1776, of the pro-independence monograph *Common Sense*. The pamphlet went on to sell 500,000 copies in the six months following its publication, and was to prove instrumental in the drafting of the *Declaration Of Independence* and in fomenting an 'open' rather than a 'concealed' movement towards the American colonies' eventual fracture with the mother country.

It would be pleasant to contrive a reading of the 'three sisters' in line 2 as referring to the Three Sisters Lighthouse, on Nauset Beach, near Eastham, Cape Cod, whose lights (if they had been built in time) might well have guided Thomas Paine towards the estate at New Rochelle that George Washington had been instrumental in granting him – another odd coincidence finds the lighthouses located near the Old Eastham Windmill, itself built by another Thomas Paine, in Plymouth, in 1680. But prudence, however, dictates that the three sisters (as well as suggesting the Three Fates, Clotho, Lachesis, and Atropos) are probably those of Elizabeth Monroe (*la belle Americaine*), wife of James Monroe (the American Minister to France and later fifth US President), who nursed Paine back to health after his eleven-month incarceration in the Luxembourg Prison – he had fallen foul of Robespierre, and James Monroe had won his release – and as a result of whose ministrations he was able to complete the second part of *The Age Of Reason*.

The last two lines of the quatrain are surely self-evident,

and deal with the subsequent influence on world events which Paine's concept of the US, and its *Lingua Franca*, English, have contrived.

Summary

A magnificent quatrain dealing with the American Revolution, and the subsequent influence of the United States, and its given language, English, on world affairs.

THE FRENCH REVOLUTION

14 JULY 1789

10/89

De brique en marbre seront les murs reduits

Sept et cinquante annees pacifiques,

Joie aux humains renoué Laqueduict,

Santé, grandz fruict joye et temps melifique.

The walls of small residences will go from brick to marble

Seven and fifty peaceful years

Joy to all humans, and the aqueduct ('that which was said') renewed

Health, fruitfulness, joy and honeyed times.

In the context of this quatrain, we must take the word *reduits* exactly as written – in Old French it means a small house or habitation, rather than the more customary 'reduced' (particularly when related to 'bricks and marble'). This relatively minor change then provides us with a major key to the quatrain, which is seen to lie in the concept of equality – i.e. on this day even small houses will be built to the same standards as palaces, and 'all humans' (and not merely the elite) will know joy.

Now to the index date of 89. And where does that take us? Why, to the exact start of the French Revolution and to the Fall of the Bastille, on the 14th July 1789, symbols of an uprising designed to achieve exactly those ends delineated in Nostradamus's quatrain. And why has no one noticed the revolutionary connection before? Because generations of Nostradamian commentators have categorically refused to pay any attention at all to Nostradamus's own index dates, maintaining that he purposely muddied the waters to throw off the Inquisition. But why bother to throw off the Inquisition when you are going to be dead decades, and sometimes even hundreds of years before the quatrains are ever proved? Is that remotely logical? Of course not.

Back to the index dates. What happens if we add 1789 to the 'seven and fifty peaceful years' mentioned in line 2? We come to 1846, and the escape of Louis Napoleon (ironically disguised as a labourer) from the fortress of Ham, in the department of the Somme, to which he had been condemned for life in 1840, for insurrection. This escape led directly to the February Revolution of 1848, a popular revolution that overthrew the monarchy of Louis Philippe and established the disastrous Second Republic, under the dictatorial reign of – guess who? – Louis Napoleon (joint fomenter, with Bismarck, of the 1870-71 Franco-Prussian War, which brought about his downfall).

Summary

Nostradamus describes the *Liberté Égalité Fraternité* concept of the 1789 French Revolution, and accurately pinpoints its eventual demise under the totalitarian regime of Louis Napoleon, only to be resuscitated, and improved on, under the aegis of the modern French State.

THE MARQUIS DE LA FAYETTE

Feu couleur d'or du ciel en terre veu:
Frappé du hault, nay, fait cas merveilleux:
Grand meurtre humain; prinse du grand nepveu,
Morts d'expectacles eschappé l'orgueilleux.

A fire the colour of gold is seen in the sky

Struck from above, born, a marvel occurs

Much human slaughter; the great man's descendant is taken

The proud one escapes death thanks to a spectacular frolic.

Une échappée means a 'prank' or a 'frolic' in Old French, and not simply an 'escape', so I use both meanings here, which I believe is how Nostradamus meant the word to be taken. It certainly adds a lustre to the quatrain, suggesting, as it does, that the earth ('the proud one') may have escaped destruction by a meteor ('a fire the colour of gold') by the merest of whiskers. *Nepveu* (*neveu*), too, can mean either a 'nephew', or, more generally, a 'descendant', and I have chosen the second meaning, given the movements from above to below delineated in the first two lines of the quatrain – 'descendant', or something which descends, is merely a continuation of that conceit.

As far as the literal (as opposed to metaphorical) meaning of the quatrain goes, I believe it to be a profound meditation on the actual construct of the French Republic, and of the narrow escape France had from the Jacobin 'meteor'. The index date of 92 gives us our first clue, pointing directly towards the French Revolution, and, in particular, to the person of Marie-Joseph-Paul-Yves-Roch Gilbert, Marquis de La Fayette, a heroic figure on both sides of the Atlantic, and a moderate constitutional monarchist, who nevertheless fought all his life for freedom and equality under a tolerant and culturally enlightened hierarchy (de La Fayette was, for instance, the man who unsuccessfully tried to persuade his friend, George Washington, to free his slaves – he was also behind the design of the French tricolore, which sees the red and blue colours of Paris harmonising with the royal white).

De La Fayette was declared a traitor in 1792 by the Legislative (Constituent) Assembly, following his decision to order the national guard to open fire on the mob in the Champ de Mars (they were calling for the death of the king and queen), and for his later proposal to use the army in an attempt to restore a limited form of monarchy. As a further addition to the brew, the 'great man's descendant is taken' reference in line 3 is a direct allusion to Louis XIV's descendant, Louis XVI, being 'taken' after his flight to Varennes the previous year, at a time when de La Fayette was in charge of the national guard (and therefore a good deal more than nominally in charge of the prisoner).

With his life in imminent danger, therefore, de La Fayette was forced to flee to Liège, where he himself was 'taken' by the Prussians, and later by the Austrians, who imprisoned him for five years for his role as one of the prime movers of the French Revolution. Despite all his many reservations about de La Fayette, Napoleon later contrived the great man's release, and at his death in 1834, the in many ways Confucian de La Fayette was considered by many to be the embodiment of tolerant liberal opinion, and of the enlightened and ethical use of privilege.

Summary

A superb quatrain comparing the French Revolution to a meteor that merely grazes the earth without actually destroying it. The second part of the quatrain describes the career of the much-loved Marquis de La Fayette, who consistently refused to abuse the power he had been accorded by virtue of his birth, his great wealth, and his political acumen.

THE BATTLE OF CAPE ST VINCENT

14 FEBRUARY 1797

9/97

De mer copies en trois parts divisees,

A la seconde les vivres failleront,

Desesperez cherchant champs Helisees,

Premier en breche entrez victoire auront.

The naval force will be divided into three parts

The second wing will lack supplies

In desperation they will search for the Champs-Élysées

The first ones at the breach will have the victory.

The Elysian Fields (or in Hesiod's terms, the Isles of the Blessed) were traditionally situated on the outermost western reaches of the earth, where they were home to fallen heroes and virtuous warriors, who would live on to enjoy immortal bliss at the hands of the gods – in Nostradamus's time, however, the Champs-Élysées consisted of fields and market gardens, providing homemade produce for the Parisian markets. Both of these clues, as we shall see, are of crucial importance in interpreting this quatrain, which has previously been falsely ascribed to any number of other naval engagements, including Trafalgar.

The Portuguese Cabo de Säo Vicente (Cape of St Vincent) is at the extreme southwestern reach of Europe, and has been considered sacred to the gods since Neolithic times – in fact the Greeks and Romans knew it as the 'holy promontory', and it was taboo to spend even one night there, for fear of antagonising the Oestriminis (serpent people), who called this land of the extreme west (or *Finis Terrae*) their home. On the 14th February 1797 (*note* the perfect correlation with Nostradamus's index date), the British and the Spanish fought a decisive naval engagement there, whose effect was to keep Napoleon's Spanish allies blockaded in their harbours for the next few years (until the 1802 Peace of Amiens) and to form an effective split between France and Spain, thereby frustrating Napoleon's long-term plan (which was dependent on Spanish naval aid) of invading Britain.

The Spanish fleet, under Don José de Cordoba, had intended to join with the French fleet at Brest, to create an unstoppable force to counter the much smaller British

Mediterranean fleet – an unexpected Levanter (easterly wind) soon drove the Spanish fleet off course, however. Sir John Jervis's British Mediterranean fleet took full advantage of this fact, and while the Spanish were vainly looking around for their French allies ('in desperation they will search for the Champs-Élysées'), Jervis, having received word of the Spanish fleet's whereabouts (but not its size) from Nelson, decided to attack – he was therefore horrified to discover, at the very last moment, that he was outnumbered two to one. Nelson, scenting disaster, decided to disobey orders, and after Jervis's main fleet had effectively split the Spanish fleet in two ('the naval force will be divided into three parts'), he broke formation and pursued the larger, rather than the smaller, Spanish group. He was now in front of the Spanish, and a sitting duck. Jervis, to his credit, saw what Nelson was about, and cut his jib accordingly. Nelson's ship, the *Captain*, had as many as six Spanish ships firing down upon her at the worst moment in the battle, but at this point Nelson did an extraordinary thing – he got up close to the Spanish 80-gun *San Nicolás*, and boarded her. Then, using the almost unholy sense of initiative which was to stand him in such good stead eight years later, at Trafalgar, he crossed the *San Nicolás*'s deck with his men behind him, and boarded, via her, the 112-gun *San José*, which had become entangled with her rigging. This trick, of crossing one boat to board another, instantly became known as 'Nelson's patent bridge for boarding enemy vessels' by an admiring and grateful Royal Navy.

Summary

Nostradamus describes, to a tee, the crucial British victory
at the Cabo de Säo Vicente, which constituted unmitigated
good news for the British people, truncating, as it did, in
one fell swoop, all Napoleon's plans for an invasion of the
British mainland.

TOUSSAINT L'OUVERTURE & HAÏTIAN INDEPENDENCE

1803

7 / 3

Apres de France la victoire navale

Les Barchinons, Saillinons, les Phocens,

Lierre d'or, l'enclume serré dedans la basle

Ceux de Ptolon au fraud seront consens.

After France's naval victory

The no-boaters, the non-starters, and the no-hopers

The golden ivy, the anvil fixed inside a ball

Ptolon's men are party to the fraud.

The index date is the key here, for it applies to the year 1803, when French forces were finally defeated at the Battle of Vertières, bringing to an end the twelve-year Haïtian Slave Revolution (the Republic was actually declared liberated on the 1st January 1804). Napoleon had sent General Leclerc to Haïti in 1802 at the head of a fleet of seventy warships, and the French had, in consequence, achieved their military and naval successes ('after France's naval victory') through sheer force of numbers. The defeat at Vertières, however, marked the categorical end of nineteenth-century French colonial interference in Haïti's affairs.

Further evidence that Nostradamus is writing about Haïti comes in line 4, with the coded name of Ptolon – if we take the first two syllables (and pronounce them in the French way) we discover that they relate to the great black Haïtian military commander, Toussaint L'Ouverture [To-Lo], who had been deceived by false guarantees ('Ptolon's men are party to the fraud'), seized by Leclerc's men, and shipped off to France, where he died in captivity at the Fort du Joux, in the Jura mountains, on the 7th April 1803.

A further clue to the Haïtian connection comes at the end of line 2, with the mention of the Phocens. Phocensian Despair means desperation which terminates in victory, and stems from the days of Philip, king of Macedon, when the men of Phocis stood alone against the united might of all their enemies. In desperation, they built an enormous pyre, meaning to immolate themselves, and their women and children, upon it. Having nothing left to lose, they then threw themselves in one final, despairing act, upon the foe,

and, extraordinarily, beat them off. A similar miracle
occurred in Haïti, following the death of Toussaint
L'Ouverture.

Having taken command of the slave army, Toussaint's
lieutenant, Jean-Jacques Dessalines, withdrew them to the
former British redoubt above the village of Petite Rivière
('little river' – ergo the 'no-boaters'). With a slave army of
1,200 men, he then faced off against Leclerc's 12,000 seasoned
soldiers. Following an extraordinary series of unsuccessful
assaults (the 'non-starters'), fever in the French ranks, and a
Joan of Arc moment in which Jeanne Marie, wife of slave
brigade commander Lamartinière, appeared on the parapets
of the redoubt wearing a Phrygian cap, sash, and raised rifle
(just like Republican France's Marianne icon), Dessalines
mounted a daring bayonet raid on the French lines, ensuring
that all his remaining men and their families could escape to
fight another day.

Summary

An extraordinary quatrain detailing the events leading up
to Haïti's Declaration of Independence on the 1st January
1804, triggered by the death, in French captivity, of slave hero
Toussaint L'Ouverture in 1803. The first independent black
republic, Häiti became the blueprint for the later decoloni-
sation of numerous other countries occupied by European
powers.

THE EXISTENCE OF SLAVERY QUESTIONED

24 AUGUST 1814

7/14

Faulx exposer viendra topographie,
Seront les cruches des monuments ouvertes:
Pulluler secte saincte philosophie,
Pour blanches, noires, et pour antiques vertes.

They will come and expose the false topography

The urns of the monuments will be opened

Sects, saints, and philosophy will pullulate

For whites, blacks, and ancient greens.

Faux is an interesting word, and can mean either false (as in deceitful), or scythes. *Cruches*, too, can mean either urns (as in pitchers) or fools. Nostradamus enjoys such ambivalences, and almost certainly designed them to obfuscate, and to tantalise his readers with myriad perspectives. In line 4 *vertes*, meaning green or young, finds itself allied with ancient, as in the age old French expression '*Cet homme est encore vert*', meaning 'That man is enjoying a green old age'. The real key to the quatrain, however, lies in line 4, with the words 'white' and 'black'. Given the index date of 14, and the destruction of monuments, the quatrain can only refer to the destruction, by the British (under the aegis of the war of 1812) of Washington DC, the newly formed capital of the United States (it was formally named in 1791). The destruction of Washington's public buildings (the Senate, the Library of Congress, the House of Representatives and the United States Treasury in particular) was in revenge for the destruction by the Americans of what are now the cities of Ontario and Toronto, following the Battle of York in 1813.

At the time of the attack, Washington's population numbered 6,700 'whites', and 1,300 'blacks' – the first shot of the 1775 American Revolution ('the shot heard around the world') occurred, of course, at Lexington Green, and many of the earliest US revolutionary flags were not, in fact, red, white, and blue, but 'green', to symbolise hope. Interestingly, after the end of the war, in 1815, John Quincy Adams (later to become sixth US President) complained that British naval commanders had violated the terms of the Treaty of Ghent (which established the principle of *status quo ante bellum* –

i.e. no territorial concessions made by either side whatsoever) by refusing to return American slaves captured during the war – a logical procedure on the part of the British, however, who no longer recognised slaves as private property following the William Wilberforce initiated United Kingdom Abolition of Slavery Act of the 25th March 1807.

Summary

Following the declaration of war on Britain by the United States in 1812 (in a bid to gain further territory, most notably in Canada, but nominally on account of sovereignty violations), the British riposted with a successful propaganda-motivated attack on the US Capital City of Washington DC. This coincidentally led to the questioning of certain formerly entrenched US attitudes to slavery.

THE DISCOVERY OF THE *VENUS DE MILO*

1820

7/20

Ambassadeurs de la Toscane langue,

Avril et May Alpes et mer passer:

Celuy de veau expousera harangue,

Vie Gauloise ne venant effacer.

Tuscan-speaking ambassadors

Will cross the alps and the sea in April and May

The man of calf (scholar) will contrive a speech

The French way of life will not be rubbed out.

This is a complicated quatrain which, given the index date of 20, most probably relates to two famous Venuses – the *Medici Venus* (first century BC) and the *Venus de Milo* (circa 130 BC), which, between them, just about summed up the cultural dissimilarities (not to mention divergent aspirations) between post-Revolutionary France and Risorgimento Italy. The 'man of calf' mentioned in line 3 strengthens this reading, as it almost certainly refers to a bookish man (i.e. a scholar), and stems from the fact that most books at the period Nostradamus was writing in were covered in calf hide or vellum.

First, the *Medici Venus*, source for Botticelli's masterpiece *The Birth Of Venus* (1483). The year is 1815 and the French, humiliated after the defeat at Waterloo, are diplomatically forced to return the statue (looted by Napoleon) to the Italians via the intercession of a group of 'Tuscan-speaking ambassadors' – the *Venus* is dutifully replaced in her sconce in the Tribuna of the Uffizi gallery in Florence (regional capital of Tuscany). At that time the *Medici Venus* was universally acknowledged as possibly the greatest of all classical sculptures, and the French scholastic establishment felt its loss bitterly. Added to all that, the return of the *Medici Venus* appeared to epitomise the belittling of France as a major world power, symbolised by the exile of Napoleon to St Helena (he was to die a year after the index date of this quatrain, in 1821). Clearly something had to be done.

One night in 1820, in answer to France's prayer, a Greek peasant named Yorgos Kentrotas set out to loot some stone from amongst the ruins of the ancient city of Milos. To his surprise he came across a massive statue, broken into two pieces. Fearing its almost certain theft by the Turkish authorities if he declared it, Kentrotas hid the statue in an underground cavern. It was impossible to keep such a find secret for long, however, and the authorities soon took possession. A French naval officer, Jules Dumont d'Urville, recognised the quality of the statue and arranged for its purchase by the French ambassador, the Marquis de Rivière, on behalf of the French state. After a few further vicissitudes (including its temporary sale to a munificent priest, who intended to offer it as a gift to the Sultan of Constantinople's court translator), the great statue was formally presented to King Louis XVIII in 1821, from where it eventually came to the Louvre.

Summary

A happy tale of two Venuses and the struggle over their ownership. All ends well for the French, however, who succeed in snatching the *Venus de Milo* (at the last possible moment) from the Sultan of Constantinople, thus restoring French dignity and prestige.

SOUTH AMERICAN INDENPENDENCE

1821

4/21

Le changement sera fort difficile:
Cité, province au change gain fera:
Coeur haut, prudent mis, chassé lui habile.
Mer, terre, peuple son estat changera.

The change will be very difficult

Both the city and the province will profit by it

A great hearted man, prudently placed, will be forced to flee by a cunning one

Sea, land and peoples – their condition will change.

The year 1821 was a crucial one for South America, and saw many changes, mostly for the better. The sequence began with Simón Bolívar's defeat of a Spanish army at Carabobo, triggering both Venezuela and Ecuador's independence. A month later Peru then declared its own independence under the 'great hearted' General José de San Martín, whose subsequent voluntary resignation in 1822, after a disagreement with the 'cunning' and bulldozing *El Libertador* (Bolívar), allowed Bolívar to assume control of the country. San Martín was forced into exile ('forced to flee') in 1824, and died, still in exile, in Boulogne, in 1850. Although Bolívar's name is endemic in South America to this day, many people nevertheless consider San Martín the greater man, a feeling echoed in Arturo Luzzatt and Segundo M Argarañaz's 'Anthem to the Liberator General San Martín', the last line of which runs as follows:

> San Martín, el señor en la guerra, por secreto
> designio de Dios,
> Grande fue cuando el sol lo alumbraba, y más
> grande en la puesta del Sol.

> San Martín, master of war, and through the
> secret design of God,
> Great was he when the sun shone on him, and
> even greater when it set.

In September 1821, Guatemala, Honduras, El Salvador and Costa Rica all declared independence from Spain, with

Panama following suit in December, when it merged with the province of Great Columbia. These changes had a profound effect on the future history of the whole of Latin America, making this one of Nostradamus's most successful and upbeat quatrains.

Summary

A masterful quatrain depicting South America's long-standing struggle for independence from Spain in the nineteenth century, with a particular emphasis on the often under-appreciated national liberator, General José de San Martín.

CHARLES DARWIN

La Lune au plain de nuict sus (sur) le haut mont
Le nouveau sophe d'un seul cerveau la (l'a) veu:
Par ses disciples estre immortel semond,
Yeux au mydi, en seins mains, corps au feu.

The full moon will be seen at night on the high mountain

By the solitary, newly-fledged scholar

Thanks to his disciples, his teachings become immortal

His eyes turned to the southern hemisphere, hands on chest, they immolate his body.

On the 27th December 1831, the recently graduated (Cambridge: January 1831) Charles Darwin, made his way up the gangplank of HMS *Beagle*, and towards the Galapagos Islands, the southern hemisphere, and a unique place in the history of science and of humanity. As a result of his five-year voyage in the *Beagle*, Darwin posited that species originated through evolutionary change, natural selection, and common descent, rather than, by inference, through divine intervention or the catastrophe theory. His 1859 book *On The Origin Of Species* has since proved to be one of the single most influential books of the nineteenth century, and disciples of Darwinism such as John Burdon Haldane, Sewell Wright, Julian Huxley and Richard Dawkins, have fanned the flames of evolutionary theory ever since.

Author's Note: In view of line 4, it might be interesting to point out that the first formal cremation in the United States took place in Washington, Pennsylvania, on the 6th December 1876 – the body was that of Baron Joseph Henry Louis Charles de Palm, and its immolation was accompanied by readings from Charles Darwin and from the Hindu Scriptures.

SUMMARY

Nostradamus correctly describes Darwin's theory of evolutionary change in terms of a gradual revelation from darkness into light, triggered by his researches and passion for the southern hemisphere.

THE FOUNDATION OF THE MODERN GREEK STATE

1832

1 / 32

Le grand empire sera tost translaté,

En lieu petit, qui bien tost viendra croistre:

Lieu bien infime d'exigue comté,

Ou au milieu viendra poser son sceptre.

The great empire will soon be turned

Into a smaller place, which will very soon begin to grow

The lowest place of an already small county

In the middle of which he will place his sceptre.

Given Nostradamus's index date of 32, it would appear that this quatrain deals with the tumultuous events surrounding the formation of the new kingdom of Greece, following the Greek War of Independence, a.k.a. the Greek Revolution (1821–31) – the revolution during which Lord Byron lost his life as a result of fever, at Messolonghi, in 1824. The 'great empire' is that of the Ottoman Turks (1299–1923), an empire that spanned, at its height, Anatolia, much of South Eastern Europe as far as the Caucasus (including Hungary, the Balkans and Poland/Lithuania), the Middle East, and considerable parts of North Africa. The July 1832 Treaty of Constantinople made of Greece (Hellas) a free country, and the very first subject state of the Ottoman Empire to win its independence.

Following the assassination of Capodistrias (the first head of state of independent Greece) in 1831, the Great Powers strove to unify Greece under one kingly family. The crown was first offered to Leopold I of Belgium, who refused it on territorial grounds – the London Conference of 1832 was then convened and the 'sceptre' offered to the seventeen-year-old Otto von Wittelsbach, a member of the ancient Bavarian princely family, and the second son of Ludwig I, king of Bavaria. The words 'which will very soon begin to grow' in line 2 most probably refer to the fact that the original demarcation lines of Greece only incorporated about a third of the Greek-speaking inhabitants of the Ottoman Empire, laying the road open to inevitable further expansion of the Greek remit at a later date.

Summary

A quatrain detailing the almost miraculous moment, in 1832, when Greece became a sovereign state, having finally succeeded in winning its independence from the toils of the Ottoman Empire.

THE *AMISTAD* CASE

2 JULY 1839

5 / 26

La gent esclave par un heur martial
Viendra en haut degré tant esleuee:
Changeront prince, naistre un provincial,
Passer la mer copie aux monts levee.

The enslaved race will, through warfare

Become elevated to such a degree

That they will change their prince for a bumpkin

An army recruited in the mountains will cross
the sea.

The index date of 26 is notable in that the 4th July 1826 marked the deaths, within hours of each other, of Thomas Jefferson and John Adams, both lifelong (if expediently pragmatic) opponents of slavery – it also marked the fiftieth anniversary of the Declaration of Independence, to which they had both contributed and been founding signatories. The number 26, in the guise of the year 1626, also marked the arrival of the first slaves in New York, whilst 1926 marked the drafting of the Slavery Convention, which outlawed slavery once and for all, defining it as 'the status or condition of a person over whom any or all of the powers attaching to the right of ownership are exercised'. The Convention went on to stipulate that 'the term 'slave trade' includes all acts involved in the capture, acquisition or disposal of a person with intent to reduce him to slavery; all acts involved in the acquisition of a slave with a view to selling or exchanging him; all acts of disposal by sale or exchange of a slave acquired with a view to being sold or exchanged, and, in general, every act of trade or transport in slaves.'

All of this doesn't help us much with 'they will change their prince for a bumpkin', though, or the 'army recruited in the mountains' and which will 'cross the sea'. Or maybe it does, for surely the most famous country bumpkin of them all, and one destined to become his country's prince (i.e. president), was Abraham Lincoln. Born in a one-room log cabin in Hardin County, Kentucky – an area which he described as a 'wild region, with many bears and other wild animals still in the woods' – this self-taught frontiersman issued his Emancipation Proclamation on the 1st January

1863, asserting the freedom of all slaves living inside the Confederacy. He was assassinated a bare two years later, just as the great army that he had helped engender was about to gain a decisive victory in the Civil War.

There is one other potentially relevant connection with John Adams and 1826, though, in the form of his son, John Quincy Adams (also US president in his time), who defended the forced captives (transported slaves) of the Spanish schooner *Amistad* against charges of mutiny and murder (his major, anti-filibustering speech on the subject was said to have lasted for eight and a half hours). It was later found that Cinqué (a.k.a. Sembe Pieh) and the former slaves under his command, had lawfully defended themselves against their Cuban/Spanish kidnappers, by taking over control of the vessel that was illegally continuing their transshipment from their original home in 'the mountains' of Sierra Leone, via Cuba, and thereafter 'across the sea' to the United States. Due to the massive effect the *Amistad* case had on enlightened US public opinion, it would perhaps also be reasonable to propose that Cinqué, and the thirty-four men and boys and three girls under his leadership, did indeed constitute an 'army'.

Summary

A quatrain detailing the undoubted 'good news' of the positive knock-on effect for anti-slavery campaigners of the notorious *Amistad* case.

NAPOLEON BONAPARTE

Avant qu'advienne le changement d'empire,

Il adviendra un cas bien merveilleux,

Le champ mué, le pilier de porphyre,

Mis, translaté sus le rochier noilleux.

Before the change of empire

A marvellous circumstance will occur

The field will moult, a pillar of porphyry

Will be placed there, transforming what lies
beneath the stony rock.

The word *noyau* (whose Old French pronunciation is euphonically akin to *noilleux*) is another word for stone, giving us stone-stone, or stone kernel. There is a potential astronomical link in Old French too, as *le noyau d'une comète* is the 'nucleus of a comet'. This spatial suggestion is further pointed up by Nostradamus's use of the word 'marvellous' in line 2, implying something out of the ordinary, or beyond the everyday. Porphyry itself is a particularly hard form of igneous rock, which just happens to be purple (the colour of royalty – the word actually does mean purple in Latin), and is thus also the colour of empires. An emperor born (as opposed to coming to power in a coup) was termed *porphyrogenitus*, and would be entombed in purple (as was, for instance, Nero). This idea was carried forward by the Bonapartists who recovered the body of Napoleon I from St Helena in 1840 (*see* index date of 43), intending to immure it in a porphyry sarcophagus at Les Invalides – traditionally, however, all porphyry came from one particular quarry, the Mons Porpyritis (or Porphyry Mountain), in the Eastern Desert of Egypt, which unfortunately happened to be unavailable in 1840, and thus Finnish quartzite had to be used instead.

This all occurred before the change of empire, just as Nostradamus predicted, in the sense that the Second French Empire dates from 1852 to 1870, falling between the Second and Third Republics. The 'marvellous circumstance' thus becomes the recovery of Napoleon's remains, and his re-interment back on French soil becomes the 'transformation', if you will, of what lies beneath the stony rock into a noumenal – rather than a merely physical – monument.

Summary

A clever quatrain effectively summing up the complicated and privileged position Napoleon now holds in the French psyche. He may be both a winner and a loser, but when he lost, he lost with élan, and when he won, he conquered.

THE FOUNDATION OF THE BAHÁ'Í FAITH

1850 ONWARDS

4/50

Libra verra regner les Hesperies,
De ciel, et terre tenir la monarchie:
D'Asie forces nul ne verra peries
Que sept ne tiennent par rang la hierarchie.

Libra will see the West reign

Over both sky and land

No one will see the genius of the Asian forces

Before seven in succession have held the hierarchy.

Peri is an interesting word, for in Old French it means a Persian genius (plural genii), an elf, or possibly a fairy. Most commentators plump for *périr*, however, meaning 'to perish', but I think the Persian connection is advertent on Nostradamus's part, and to associate the word Asia automatically with defeat reflects a rather patronising modern conceit. 'Genius' in this case refers not to the 'brilliance' of the Asian forces, but rather to the 'fallen angels of Islam', which, in the Persian as opposed to the Roman reading of the word genius/genii, had a corporeal form, which could be changed at will. These angels dwelt in the imaginary country of Ginnistan/Jinnistan, under the dominion of the demon Eblis (whose name means 'despair'), and were by and large hostile to mankind, although they were occasionally constrained to work as its servant (*pace* Sinbad the Sailor and the Thief of Baghdad, etc. etc.).

With all this in mind, we now turn to the index date of 50, and find that it most probably refers to the year 1850, which saw the execution for heresy of the Shiraz born Mirza Ali Mohammed (founder of the Islamic Babi sect), in Tabriz, Persia, on the 9th July, at the behest of the Shia clerical establishment. His follower, Mirza Husayn Ali, immediately declared himself the divine prophet foretold by his predecessor, triggering the formation of the Bahá'í faith. Considered an Islamic heresy in fundamentalist circles (the 'fallen angel' connection), the generally peaceable Bahá'í have encountered considerable discrimination in post-revolutionary Iran, and it is hard, at this stage, to suggest that they might be in for a resurgence (they have only some 5 million worldwide adherents at last count).

Interestingly, however, there is one further clue to the Bahá'í connection held within the quatrain, and that is line 4's statement 'before seven in succession have held the hierarchy' – for the Bahá'í faith happens to believe that Seven Valleys describe the path to union with God, and that the seven founders of the world's main religions – namely Abraham, Moses, Krishna, Buddha, Zoroaster, Jesus Christ and Mohammed – are all divine teachers sent to educate and guide humanity on its eventual path towards enlightenment.

Summary

An intricate quatrain dealing with the events that led up to the eventual formation of the Bahá'í faith, circa 1866.

CAIRO & THE END OF EMPIRE

1882

9 / 82

Par le deluge et pestilence forte
La cité grande de long temps assiegee,
La sentinelle et garde de main morte,
Subite prinse, mais de nul oultragee.

By flood and powerful corruption

The great city finds itself, for a long time,
besieged

Both the sentry and the bodyguard are dead

Sudden capture, but no one of consequence
is affronted.

The index date of 9/82 correlates perfectly with the 1882 British Occupation of Cairo, which took place on the 15th September (the ninth month), following a lengthy series of arguments over the future of the Suez Canal and of Egypt's national debt. Anti-European riots had broken out earlier that year, leading to a bombardment of Alexandria by ships of the British Royal Navy. This led to what is now called the Anglo-Egyptian War of 1882, which saw British forces facing up to an Egyptian army led by Colonel Ahmad Urabi (a.k.a. Urabi Pasha), which culminated in Urabi's defeat at the battle of Tel el-Kebir (following a five-week 'siege' at Zagazig).

The phrase 'no one of consequence is affronted' may refer either to the Khedive Tawfiq, who might conceivably have viewed the British defeat of 'the upstart' Urabi as something of a convenience (for it led to his reinstatement as Khedive twelve days later), or to the fact that Lord Dufferin, the British ambassador in Constantinople (and British commissioner in Egypt), stepped in when the Khedive condemned Urabi to death, and saw that the sentence was commuted merely to one of exile. As a result of this, Urabi was sent to the then British Colony of Ceylon, where he died peacefully in 1911.

SUMMARY

Nostradamus gives a brief description, with an exact index date, of the 1882 British occupation of Cairo, which eventually stretched all the way to 1956, and mirrored the largely peaceful ending of the British Empire.

SUBJECT

THE MAHDI

DATE

1884/1885

QUATRAIN

1/84

Lune obscurecie aux profondes tenebres,

Son frère passe de couleur ferrugine:

Le grand caché long temps soubz les tenebres,

Tiedera fer dans la pluie sanguine.

The moon is hidden by deep shadows

Her brother, the sun, changes to blood colour

The great man is hidden by the shadows for a
long time

They will warm their steel in the bloody rain.

Well, there's good news and then there's 'good news'. This was good news for the Mahdi and his band of holy warriors, as they struggled, between March 12th 1884 and January 26th 1885, to successfully invest Khartoum. Considered a great man by his followers, the Mahdi had retired to a cave ('the great man is hidden by the shadows') after his defeat before Omdurman, to await divine guidance from Allah. He returned with the news that Allah had declared sixty days of rest following which 'blood would flow like water' – the battle of Abu Klea, almost exactly sixty days later, was to prove him right.

Nostradamus's mention of the 'moon' in line 1, and his reiteration of the word 'shadows', further strengthens the Mahdi reading, as the moon, in the form of a crescent, was the symbol of Ottoman Islam (derived, originally, from the Carthaginian goddess Tanit, and taken on by the Muslims after the fall of Constantinople in 1453). Thanks to perfidy on the part of General Gordon's Egyptian Lieutenant, Faraz Pasha, the gates of Khartoum were opened to the Mahdi's forces on the 26th January 1885, and General Gordon was surprised on his way to the Austrian consulate, shot, and his head spitted on a spear and paraded around the city ('they will warm their steel in the bloody rain'). The Mahdi didn't have much time to enjoy the fruits of his victory, however, for he succumbed to typhus that same year.

SUMMARY

The successful investiture by the Sufi-influenced Mahdi and his forces of the city of Khartoum, in 1885.

FIN DE SIÈCLE

1900

3/100

Entre Gaulois le dernier honoré.
D'homme ennemi sera victorieux:
Force et terroir en moment exploré,
D'un coup de traict quand mourra l'enuieux.

Among the French the last is honoured

The enemy of man will be victorious

Both strength and terroir will eventually be explored

The tiresome one will die from a traitor's bullet (bowshot).

This quatrain strikes me as outside the usual run of Nostradamus's verses, as nothing in it really seems to hold together. Given its index date of 100, therefore, and its position at the end of a *Century* series, I believe it to be a summing up of the year 1900, with each line destined to be taken separately. Let's take the quatrain in reverse order then, as the fourth line, which would appear to depict an assassination, would also seem to offer us the greatest number of clues.

The main political assassination to take place in 1900 occurred on the 29th July, when Italian anarchist Gaetano Bresci shot King Umberto I at Monza four times, precipitating a constitutional crisis in which the deeply unpopular ('tiresome') king was succeeded by his son, Victor Emmanuel III (later to die in exile in Egypt). *Terroir*, in line 3, is a peculiarly French word, meaning more than soil (in the sense of being quasi-locational), and less than homeland – a good translation might be the savour, or taste, of one's own country. In France, 1900 saw the working day limited, in the case of women and children, to a maximum of eleven hours, and also the imposition of a gun on every policeman – but I've a strange feeling that 'both strength and *terroir* will eventually be explored' is more likely to refer to the commissioning, by André and Edouard Michelin, producers of the famous French tyre, of the now world-famous Guide Michelin, which has indeed gone on to explore every conceivable highway and byway of French life, both residentially, culinarily and viticulturally.

'The enemy of man' in line 2 may refer to Vladimir Ilyich

Ulyanov, otherwise known as Lenin, who was released from three years of exile in Siberia on the 29th January 1900, and went on to overturn all accepted norms in Russia, whilst 'amongst the French the last is honoured' is a conceivable reference to the Paris *Exposition Universelle* of 1900, which was specifically designed to 'celebrate the achievements of the past century, and accelerate development into the next'. Yes I know all this is tendentious in the extreme – but it does fit rather neatly into the text.

Summary

Nostradamus celebrates the *Fin De Siècle* in his own End Of Century quatrain, suggesting that flux often comes before positive change for the good.

ALBERT EINSTEIN'S
ANNUS MIRABILIS

1905

3 / 5

Pres loing defaut de deux grands luminaires,

Qui surviendra entre l'Avril et Mars

O quel cherté! Mais deux grans debonnaires,

Par terre et mer secourrant toutes pars.

Two great luminaries, both near and far, are blemished

This will occur some time between April and March

Oh what a terrible cost! But two great gentlemen

Will assist all parties, both by land and sea.

The two great luminaries are the sun (far) and the moon (near), so we can assume, when Nostradamus talks of a blemish, that he is implying both an eclipse and an alchemical *Conjunctio* that has gone slightly wrong (i.e. the sulphur and the mercury have failed to mix). Given the index date of 3/5, it seems that the eclipse Nostradamus is referring to, and that occurred between April and March of the following year, must be the total solar eclipse of the 30th August 1905. A member of Saros 143, the eclipse began in Canada, and tracked the Atlantic, then crossed parts of Spain and North Africa. The greatest duration, of three minutes and forty-six seconds, occurred over northern Spain. The Abbé Théophile Moreux, who viewed the eclipse at Sfax, in Tunisia, describes it thus:

> At the appointed hour, the two kings of the skies
> embraced each other, then, little by little, the
> moon, with her black disk, ate the brilliant star
> of the day. 'The Corona! The Corona!' my
> companions shouted. More than an hour was to
> pass before the lunar breakfast was completed.

Now given the date, 1905, and Nostradamus's concern, in the quatrain, with both alchemy and light, we find ourselves inexorably led towards Albert Einstein – for 1905 was known as his *annus mirabilis*, on account of the two great papers he published, on March 17th and June 30th respectively, and that were to lay the groundwork for quantum physics. The first paper was entitled 'On a heuristic viewpoint concerning the production and transformation of light', by means of which Einstein explains the photoelectric effect using the notion of light quanta – the second paper was 'On the Electrodynamics of Moving Bodies', in which he discovered special relativity. In the interim, of course, he had also found the time to submit his doctoral dissertation (May 11th 1905) 'On the Motion of Small Particles', in which he explains the Brownian Motion.

But Nostradamus speaks of 'two great gentlemen', surely? Well the other must surely be Albert Einhorn, the eminent German chemist who first effectively synthesised procaine hydrochloride, in 1905, which he immediately patented under the name Novocain, and which is still in use today as a non-addictive dental anaesthetic. Between them, these two great gentlemen, modern scions of a noble line of historical alchemists, most certainly assisted 'all parties, both by land and sea'.

Summary

Nostradamus connects the great solar eclipse of 1905 with Albert Einstein's *annus mirabilis*, and the discovery, by Albert Einhorn, of the wonder drug Novocain.

THE MODERN ERA BEGINS

9 NOVEMBER 1918

6 / 18

Par les phisiques le grand Roy delaissé,
Par sort non art de l'Ebrieu est en vie:
Lui et son genre au regne hault poussé,
Grace donnee à gent qui Christ enuie.

The great king is forsaken by his philosophers

Despite his ebriety (drunkenness) he still lives

He and his kind are pushed high in the realm

Grace is accorded to those who anger God.

Most commentators translate *Ebrieu* in line 2 as Hebrew (possibly influenced by Bible memories of Nebuchadnezzar's dream), but it is more likely to mean ebriety, or drunkenness (which in seventeenth-century chimerical physics was also used metaphorically as any condition leading to 'ultra-violent catastrophe'). Similarly, in line 1, *phisiques* is usually mistranslated as physicians, whereas *physique* in Old French means natural philosophy, or physics. These readings accord far more with the general run of the quatrain, which appears to portray a monarch who has gone to the bad, and who has been given up on by his advisers.

Given the index date of 18, therefore, we are inexorably drawn to the year 1918, which saw Kaiser Wilhelm II of Germany advised by his deputy chief of staff, General Erich Ludendorff, that the Great War was lost. This occurred on the 29th September, and on the 8th November following, the Kaiser abdicated, effectively ending the 1,000-year-old ruling Hohenzollern dynasty – he was allowed to retreat into exile, however, in Holland ('he still lives'), rather than be held accountable for the 'war to end all wars' allegedly fought in his name. That same year also saw the end of the Hapsburg and Romanov dynasties, with the effective abdication of Emperor Charles I of Austria, and the execution, at Ekaterinburg, of the Russian tsar and his entire family.

SUMMARY

Historically 1918 was the year that saw the greatest ever swing from monarchism to republicanism – good news for iconoclasts, then, and the true beginning of the modern era.

THE SCOPES MONKEY TRIAL

25 MAY 1925

1/25

Perdu, trouvé, caché de si long siecle
Sera pasteur demi dieu honore,
Ainsi que la lune achève son grand cycle
Par autres veux sera deshonoré.

Lost, found, hidden for so many centuries

The pastor will be honoured as a demigod

Just as the moon completes her great cycle

Others will wish to disgrace him.

Many commentators leap with glee onto the Louis Pasteur (1822–95) bandwagon when faced with this quatrain – after all, the word *pasteur* is clearly used in line 2, and therefore the French father of microbiology must surely be the demigod referred to in the text? Well, mustn't he?

Actually, no. To a person of Nostradamus's generation, the word *pasteur* would have had the clear meaning of a Protestant minister, stemming, as it does, from the French word for 'shepherd'. With this in mind, and given the index date of 25, a far more interesting reading of the quatrain comes to light. For May 1925 saw the infamous Scopes Monkey Trial, in which lawyers Clarence Darrow and William Henry Bryan faced up to each other in the unlikely setting of the Rhea county courthouse in Dayton, Tennessee, to dispute the legitimacy or not of teaching Darwin's Theory of Evolution to young children. Baptist pastor William Bell Riley (founder and president of the World Christian Fundamentals Association) was the driving force behind the case for the defence, and it was he and his Adamist league who secured ex-presidential candidate and Christian fundamentalist Bryan's services on behalf of the southern Bible Belt confederacy. The trial swiftly became a press bonanza, with journalistic celebrities of the ilk of H L Mencken leaping into the fray against the infamous Butler Act (which forbade the teaching of any evolutionary theory suggesting that man might be descended from a lower order of primates).

At its height the trial was covered by more than 100 US reporters, with a further phalanx from across the Atlantic, generating a cumulative telegraphy output of some 165,000 words a day. At the end of the eight-day hearing the (inevitably biased) jury took a mere nine minutes to decide in favour of the fundamentalists, and Scopes, the lame-duck defendant in the case, was fined a nominal $100 for perverting young minds with Darwinism – the conviction was later set aside, however, on appeal, due to a legal technicality. The State of Tennessee finally repealed the Butler Act in 1967, but the argument, as Nostradamus predicted, still continues.

Summary
A beautifully structured quatrain detailing the Scopes Monkey Trial of 1925 in which Darwinist lawyer Clarence Darrow (of Leopold and Loeb fame) theoretically, if not legally, trounced his fundamentalist Christian opposite number.

ALFONSO XIII

Tant d'ans les guerres en Gaule dureront,

Oultre la course du Castulon monarque

Victoire incerte trois grands couronneront

Aigle, coq, lune, lyon, soleil en marque.

The wars in France will last for so many years

Beyond the running of the Castulon king

An uncertain victory will crown the three grandees

Eagle, cock, moon, lion, the sun in its mark.

An interesting quatrain, this, which settles itself in the index year of 31 (1931), the fulcrum year between the two great wars of the twentieth century to take place on French soil ('the wars in France will last so many years'). The Castulon king in line 2 is the Spanish Castilian King Alfonso XIII who, on the 14th February 1931, was forced to leave Spain following the republican victory – considered by many to be an unofficial plebiscite on the monarchy's future – during the country's municipal elections. He was subsequently proclaimed guilty of high treason and forced to abdicate. The anarchism, anti-clericalism and iconoclasm that erupted after the elections was a direct precursor of the Spanish Civil War (17th July 1936 – 1st April 1939), which, in turn, fuelled the German belief that an all out European war might eventually result in an Axis victory.

The three grandees who benefit from the 'uncertain victory' (for Stalin's victory was more certain, surely) are, of necessity, Roosevelt/Truman, De Gaulle, and Churchill/Atlee – respectively the American 'eagle', the French 'cock' and the British 'lion'. The reason I append the Truman and Atlee names is because the 'uncertain victory' which occurs when the 'sun is in its mark' (i.e. in Leo, between 22nd July and 21st August) must of necessity suggest the 1945 Potsdam Conference (which ended on the 2nd August, and during which Churchill lost his mandate to be replaced by Atlee, and before which Roosevelt had died to be replaced by Truman) and which essentially culminated in a victory for Stalin. The sun (as in the rising sun flag, called by the Japanese *Hinomaru*, meaning 'circle of the sun') may also refer to Japan, the unacknowledged fourth party at the conference, for it was here that Truman decided on the use of the atomic bomb, which was set off on the 6th and 9th of August of that same year over Hiroshima and Nagasaki, when the sun was, indeed, 'in its mark' – Japan capitulated on the 12th August.

Summary

Good news of sorts, in that, following the precursor year of 1931, which saw the roots of the Spanish Civil War, the allies go on to win an 'uncertain victory' in the Second World War – i.e. over Germany and Japan, but not over Stalin.

THE STAVISKY AFFAIR

1934

1/34

L'oyseau de proye volant a la fenestre
Avant conflict faict aux Francoys pareure
L'un bon prendra, l'un ambigue sinistre,
La partie foyble tiendra par bon augure.

The bird of prey flying at the window

Appears to the French before the conflict commences

Some will take it favourably, others as a sinister cold collation

The weaker side will hold fast and gain the ascendancy.

Ambigue can have two possible definitions here (surprise, surprise) – the one is 'ambiguous', and the other a 'cold supper' or 'cold collation'. The second appears to be Nostradamus's meaning, bearing in mind his use of the word 'take' (as in the taking of food) in the first part of the line. Given this fact, and the categorical mention of 'the French' in line 2, together with the multitude of other clues and an index date of 34, we are inexorably led towards the Stavisky Affair, which reached its climax on the 8th January 1934.

Handsome Serge Alexandre Stavisky (*le beau Sasha*), an embezzler and dealer in fraudulent bonds, apparently committed suicide in an upper room of a Chamonix chalet following seven years of claim, counter-claim, and cover-up (he was granted bail on nineteen separate occasions) by the French Radical-Socialist Government. The alleged suicide by gunshot was widely viewed as an assassination plot by the police designed to protect high-up officials implicated in the ongoing scandal, however, and both the royalist right and the communist left took to the streets in protest during the Paris riots of the 6th and 7th February, which culminated in a crippling general strike.

Stavisky's crime was to have released hundreds of millions of francs' worth of false bonds to the city of Bayonne's municipal pawnshop – bonds which were subsequently repurchased by a series of life assurance companies which, according to Janet Flanner, the *New Yorker*'s Paris correspondent, 'were counselled by the Minister of Colonies, who was counselled by the Minister of Commerce, who was counselled by the Mayor of Bayonne, who was counselled by the little manager of the hockshop, who was counselled by Stavisky'. One would like to think that the 'bird of prey flying at the window' in line 1 represents the *flics* (cops), who constituted what certain newspapers of the period chose to call Stavisky's 'long arm' – a jocular reference to the distance the bullet had allegedly travelled before finishing off the no doubt somewhat reluctant suicidee.

Summary

Nostradamus's take on the famous Stavisky Affair, which engendered a series of riots, a putsch, and a general strike, whose ultimate result was the downfall of an extremely unpopular and corrupt French government.

THE WARTIME SPARING OF AACHEN

1941 ONWARDS

7/41

Les oz des piedz et des main enserrés,
Par bruit maison long temps inhabitee:
Seront par songes concavant deterrés,
Maison salubre et sans bruit habitee.

The bones of the feet and the hand are contained

For a long time, thanks to the noise, the house remains uninhabited

They are disinterred by hollow dreams

The healthy and peaceful house is inhabited once again.

The emperor Charlemagne (742–814), founding father of both France and Germany, and considered by many to be the father of Europe, established Aachen (Aix-La-Chapelle) as his *Roma Secunda* ('second Rome'), intending it to form the major part of his *renovatio imperii Romanorum* ('revival of the Roman Empire') project. In consequence, the imperial palace at Aachen was built on a grandiose scale, and was designed to attract artists, musicians, theologians, scholars and poets to the court of this great Frankish king – one of Jean de Longuyon's 'nine worthies' or 'perfect warriors', alongside Hector, Alexander the Great, Julius Caesar, Joshua, David, Judas Maccabaeus, King Arthur and Godfrey of Bouillon – in an extraordinarily enlightened effort to create a comparativist court school where all the liberal arts (*artes liberales*) would be taught and later disseminated to a wider world. The original Church of Our Lady (of which the famous Octagon still stands, to this day forming the central core of the remaining sequence of buildings), was without doubt the most magnificent stone edifice north of the Alps at that time.

If you leave the cathedral today, walk to the end of the street and turn immediately right, you will come to the great treasury of Aachen Cathedral, in which lie the famous relics which Nostradamus mentions in line 1. One of the primary relics (the mortal remains of saints, etc., as opposed to objects merely connected with them) is known as the Arm Reliquary, and is constructed in the form of an upraised hand (the hand that held Charlemagne's famous sword *Joyeuse*, or 'joyful', which was buried with its owner) within which the ulna and radius of Charlemagne's right forearm can be clearly seen behind a rock-crystal pane of glass. In addition there are the Three Small Reliquaries of Aachen, which purportedly contain the belt of the Virgin Mary, the belt of Jesus Christ, and the scourge with which Christ was whipped on the way to Calvary, and also the gothic Three-Tower-Reliquary, which as well as monstrancing Charlemagne's thighbone, is also said to contain a piece of the nail of the Cross, a splinter of the Cross itself, and a fragment of the Crown of Thorns. During the Middle Ages, at the time of the annual shrine pilgrimages, people would come from all over Europe to see the reliquaries, but later the custom was changed to one viewing in every seven years.

Due to the symbolic importance of Aachen to European sensibilities, it was decided, during the Second World War, that the cathedral would be specifically spared during bombing raids. To this end pathfinders were sent ahead to mark the cathedral precincts, and the (largely British) bombing crews effectively avoided destroying what Nostradamus tellingly calls the 'house' (of Europe). On the 21st October 1944 there was a massive German surrender at Aachen, which finally brought the restoration of peace so tellingly described by Nostradamus in line 4, ending, once and for all, the 'hollow dreams' of the (at least in Charlemagne's terms) 'pagan' Adolf Hitler.

Summary

An outstanding quatrain which describes the enlightened sparing of the cathedral and reliquaries of Charlemagne, founding father of Europe.

THE CITY OF LYONS

1946

3 / 46

Le ciel (de Plancus la cité) nous presaige

Par clers insignes et par estoiles fixes,

Que de son change subit s'aproche l'aage

Ne pour son bien, ne pour ses malefices.

The sky (the city of Plancus) tells us

By clear signals and by the fixed stars

That by its sudden change the age approaches

Neither for its good, nor for its bewitchment.

The good news is that there is no news – or at least that is what Nostradamus appears to be telling us. One may assume that the city he is referring to in line 1 is Lyons (Lugdunum), an area originally inhabited by the Segusians, but formally colonised and made important by the Romans under Lucius Munatius Plancus in 43 BC. Plancus, who ended up a Roman senator, was renowned – rather like the Vicar of Bray – for his expediently shifting allegiances, which saw him moving from the assassinated Julius Caesar's camp, to that of Mark Antony, to that of Octavian – something of a fair-weather friend, in other words. He is also one of the few Romans whose massive tomb (at Gaeta, near Naples, in Italy) survives intact, although it *was* rather curiously rededicated to the Virgin Mary during the nineteenth century – interestingly, of course, *cité* in Old French may also refer to a tomb or series of tombs, as in *la cité des morts*, in Cairo.

As far as the index date goes, one finds oneself in something of a quandary. 1646 was the year in which architect Simon Maupin designed and built the outstanding Lyons City Hall, which, twenty-eight years later, was partially destroyed by fire and subsequently restored by Jules Hardouin-Mansart – but that seems just a little tendentious, and one is forced to ask oneself why Nostradamus would have focused on something of so little fundamental importance (except to the Lyonnais). The year 1946, of course, saw the end of the first full year of Lyons' freedom from wartime occupation, with memories of the infamous Klaus Barbie (the butcher of Lyons) still fresh in everybody's minds – it was also the year in which the City of Lyons was awarded the French Resistance Medal.

All in all, however, the quatrain seems a generalised one, possibly referring, in the broadest possible terms, to the eventual passing of the 2,160-year-long Age of Pisces (the age of Christianity, the yin, and of war) and to the dawning of the new Age of Aquarius (the age of freedom, peace, the yang, and the water bearer), which is scheduled to start at some point between 2012 and 2600 (and possibly as late as 2654).

Summary
A quatrain that may refer either to the history of the City of Lyons, or to the eventual dawning of a new Aquarian age.

KING ABDULLAH I OF JORDAN

20 JULY 1951

6/51

Peuple assemblé voir nouveau expectacle,
Princes et Roys par plusieurs assistans:
Pilliers faillir, murs, mis comme miracle
Le Roi sauvé et trente des instans.

People assemble to see the new spectacle

Princes and Kings, with many attendants

Pillars will fall, and walls, but miraculously

The King is saved and thirty of those with him.

On the 20th July 1951, during a visit to Jerusalem to mourn the death by assassination of Riad Bey al-Solh, former prime minister of Lebanon, King Abdullah I of Jordan was himself assassinated. Known as King Abdullah the Founder, thanks to his initiation of the Jordanian kingdom, it was feared by many in the Arab League that King Abdullah was about to enter into a peace agreement with Israel. A plan was therefore hatched by Colonel Abdullah Tell, ex-military governor of Jerusalem, and Dr Musa Abdullah Husseini, a cousin of Haj Amin El Husseini, former Grand Mufti of Jerusalem, to assassinate the king as he attended Friday prayers at the holy Islamic shrine known as the Dome of the Rock (687–91). 'The King is saved' does not, for obvious reasons, refer to Abdullah himself, but to his grandson, Hussein Bin Talal (later King Hussein of Jordan), who was miraculously saved from the assassin's bullet by a medal that his grandfather had fortuitously insisted that he wear on that particular morning. The young Hussein went on to succeed his father, King Talal Bin Abdullah – who was forced to abdicate after little more than a year on account of incipient schizophrenia – reigning, in his father's stead, for a total of forty-seven years.

SUMMARY

The assassination of King Abdullah I of Jordan had the unexpected effect of propelling his sixteen-year-old grandson, Prince Hussein, into the political limelight – a position he was skilfully to maintain for a further forty-seven years.

THE DAWNING OF THE NEW AGE OF AQUARIUS

La grand perte las que feront les lettres:
Avant le cycle de Latona parfaict
Feu, grand deluge plus par ignares sceptres
Que de long siecle ne se verra refaict.

Alas, there will be a great deterioration
of learning

Before Latona's cycle is accomplished

Fire, and a deluge of ignorant rulers

For many centuries there will be no remedy.

Latona (the Greek Leto), and beloved of Zeus, was the Titan mother of the twins Artemis (goddess of childbirth) and Apollo (god of the sun, of healing, of music, and of the beneficent aspects of civilisation). The birth had not been an easy one, however, as Latona had found herself on the wrong side of Hera (wife of Zeus and queen of the gods), and no country would accept her during her quickening. She finally found sanctuary on the floating island of Ortygia (now thought to be Delos), which became, as a direct consequence of the births, permanently secured to the seabed, with Mount Cynthus, upon which the Titan-ness had rested herself during parturition, becoming a sacred place. Custom has it that after the birth the exhausted Latona (who, thanks to Hera, had not had the benefit of goddess of childbirth Eileithyia's midwifery skills) was mocked by some Lycian clowns as she bent down to drink from a nearby fountain – with Zeus's help, however, they were turned into frogs.

The year 1962 (*see* index date) saw the first ever recording of the Beatles, the debut of the Rolling Stones, the first alignment for 400 years of Neptune and the now demoted Pluto (and the concomitant seeding of the Aquarian Age due to a rare conjunction of seven solar systemic bodies on the 3rd to 5th February), major floods ('*grand deluge*') on the North Sea coasts and in Spain, the Cuban Missile Crisis, the Second Vatican Council (in which the sacred Catholic Liturgy was permanently revised), and, quite arguably, the beginning of the era of the 'common man'. I would suggest therefore that philistinism, and the downgrading of the great in favour of the mundane, is at the heart of Nostradamus's meaning here.

He foretells a time when mediocrity will rise to the fore, and in which the traditional acquisition of knowledge ('a great deterioration of learning') will give way to an idealistic but nevertheless ill-founded desire for equality – this will result in a denigration of intellectual aspiration culminating in a new dark age from which 'for many centuries there will be no remedy'.

The good news is that Latona's cycle will eventually end, and the true 'Age of Aquarius' (due around 2600, when the vernal equinox first occurs outside Pisces and in Aquarius) will begin. This period will usher in a major concatenation of religion and science (the material and the spiritual), and, at least according to Nostradamus, permanently reverse the backward trend.

Summary

Nostradamus foresees a long period of stagnation, triggered by the lauding of the mediocre and the downgrading of excellence and aesthetic discrimination – this period will end, however, circa 2600, ushering in a new, more symbiotic, age. The precursory dawning of this New Age, however, may well have occurred during the 1960s.

BEGINNINGS OF A RESURGENT CHINA

1966

9/66

Paix, union sera et changement,

Estatz, offices, bas hault, et hault bien bas,

Dresser voiage le fruict premier torment,

Guerre cesser, civils proces debatz.

There will be peace, union and change

Governments, sinecures, the low raised and the mighty lowered

A voyage is prepared, fruit of the first torment

Warfare will cease, the process of civil law is debated.

This is a curious quatrain, harking back to 'the first torment', which must surely be the fall of Adam and Eve from the Garden of Eden ('the punishment of mankind'). The voyage, therefore, must relate to the voyage undertaken by Noah's ark, which carried Adam and Eve's descendants away from danger and towards the creation of a New World, following God's one-of-a-kind decision to punish mankind's aberrant behaviour by means of a Great Flood ('the fire next time').

The obvious deduction, therefore, must be that Nostradamus is suggesting some roughly equivalent tragedy which will carry as yet unanticipated advantages in its wake – and at first glance, thanks to the index date of 9/66, he would appear to be nominating the Great Fire of London for the position, as it occurred in the ninth month (2nd to 6th September) of 1666 [see 2/51 – 1666: The Great Fire Of London]. An alternate reading might be that Nostradamus was once again predicting his own death, which occurred on the 2nd July 1566, but my own instinct is that he was pointing the way towards something more fundamental – something along the lines of Chairman Mao Zedong's 1966 Cultural Revolution, whose aim was to revivify a faltering revolutionary spirit, liberating the so-called unregenerate bourgeois from the chains of their inherited socio-economic background in order the better to reintegrate them within the class struggle (i.e. by causing 'the low to be raised and the mighty lowered' – Mao even sent soon-to-be supreme leader Deng Xiaoping to work in an engine factory, as part of his re-education).

What actually happened during the Cultural Revolution was that China descended into a virtual civil war for ten years, only emerging after Mao's death into the precursor of today's vibrant and largely forward-looking Chinese state.

Summary

An interesting quatrain which sees China's Cultural Revolution as a sort of Great Flood, acting as a direct precursor to today's more balanced and economically viable superstate.

ISABEL PERON

1 JULY 1974

6/74

La deschassee au regne tournera,

Ses ennemis trouvés des conjurés:

Plus que jamais son temps triomphera,

Trois et septante à mort trop asseurés.

The exiled woman returns to reign

Her enemies are found amongst the conspirators

Her era will be more triumphal than ever

Three and seventy are known to have died.

This is the return from exile of Isabel (Isabelita) Perón to Argentina on the 29th June 1974, following the illness of the Argentine president, her husband, Juan Perón. With her husband effectively *hors de combat*, Isabelita was elected president of Argentina in her own right on the 1st July 1974, very nearly a year to the day following the Ezeiza Massacre which succeeded in toppling Perón's predecessor and friend, Héctor Cámpora ('*El Tio*'), from power.

Isabel, a former nightclub dancer, was quite incapable of managing a state in such a complicated and dangerous condition as Argentina was at the time, and despite first receiving assurances of support from the army, she was later kidnapped, placed under house arrest for five years, and then deported to Spain by the proto-fascist clique responsible for ousting her.

SUMMARY

Nostradamus's index date leads us to Isabelita Perón, third wife of the immensely popular Juan Perón, inceptor and mouthpiece of the Argentine Peronist movement, which purported to represent a so-called 'third way' between capitalism and socialism. The arbitrary manner of Isabelita's downfall arguably paved the way for the eventual rejection of totalitarianism by the Argentine people.

NOMADISM & FREEDOM

5/76

En lieu libere tendra son pavillon,
Et ne voldra en cités prendre place:
Aix, Carpen l'isle volce, mont Cavaillon,
Par tous les lieux abolira la trasse.

He will pitch his tent in free places

Preferring to avoid cities

Aix, Carpentras, Isle-sur-la-Sorgue, Vaucluse,
Montagne Du Luberon, Cavaillon

In each place he will destroy his traces.

A simple reading of this quatrain (often the best way to approach it) instinctively takes us to the gypsy/Roma race, and to their apparently innate nomadic drive. The Roma first arrived in Germany circa 1417, and in France ten years later, so Nostradamus (1503–66) would most certainly have heard of them, and possibly even come across bands of northern French Manouche (Manush/Sinti), or southern French Gitanos (Calé), on his travels – Titian even painted a wonderful *Gypsy Madonna* in 1512, which is now resident at the Vienna Kunsthistorisches Museum.

However all the places mentioned in line 3 are also within 50 kilometres, as the crow flies, of Nostradamus's birthplace of St-Rémy-de-Provence, and one must therefore factor in a possible reference to the Wandering Jew – later known as Isaac Laquedem, by, amongst others, Alexandre Dumas – for Nostradamus came originally (before his family's Catholic integration in 1455) of Judaic stock. In both cases – that of the Wandering Jew and that of the gypsy – popular legend has it that God condemned the descendants of one particular miscreant in each tribe to perpetual nomadism, on account of the crime of *lèse majesté* towards his son, Jesus. In the case of the gypsies, it was allegedly on account of the gypsy smith who had agreed to forge the nails that were later used to attach Jesus to the Cross, and in the case of the Jews, it was allegedly on account of the taunting by a Jewish shoemaker (possibly Cartaphilus) of Jesus on the way to the Crucifixion – in each case popular legend had it that the relevant tribes were deemed to have been condemned to wander the earth until the Second Coming in collective penance for the sins of one ancestor.

Psychological logic, of course, dictates that human nature must always find excuses for its prejudices, and in the case of both the gypsies and the Jews – one has only to think of the specifically targeted pogroms during the Second World War in Nazi Germany – these myths simply provided a convenient excuse for persecution. All in all, however, it is more likely that Nostradamus was referring to the gypsy/Roma rather to the Jewish race, for the myth of the Wandering Jew was only truly encapsulated in the early part of the seventeenth century, whereas that of the gypsy smith was current at a considerably earlier period.

As far as the index date goes, it would be nice to contrive a connection between Adam Smith's *Wealth Of Nations* (1776) and his kidnap by a band of gypsies when he was four years old, but a more specific connection might be with the United Kingdom's 1976 Race Relations Act, which, for the very first time, recognised gypsies and Irish travellers as a specific ethnic group in their own right, and 'made it unlawful to discriminate against a person, directly or indirectly on racial grounds...'

Summary
Nostradamus describes the nomadic life of the gypsy/Roma tribe, possibly remembering his own travels throughout Europe and the freedoms he, in consequence, enjoyed.

KING HASSAN II

1999

4/99

L'aisné vaillant de la fille du Roy,

Repoussera si profond les Celtiques:

Qu'il mettra foudres, combien en tel arroy

Peu et loing puis profond és Hesperiques.

The valiant eldest son of the king's daughter

Will drive the Celts so far back

That he will place casks, how many, and in
so sad a plight

Few and far, then deep into the Western
marches.

This quatrain is usually wildly mistranslated, with *foudres* (plural) being taken as *foudre* (singular) meaning lightning, rather than 'large casks' or 'vats', which was its meaning in Old French – *en tel arroy* is also often translated as 'in such array', whereas it's medieval meaning suggested either 'equipment' or 'plight'. *Ès* too, in line 4, is an ancient elision of *dans les* ('in the' or 'into the'), and not some obscure Spanish borrowing designed to obfuscate and mislead the Inquisition. Frankly, even if correctly translated for a change, the quatrain still doesn't appear, on the surface at least, to make a great deal of sense – however Nostradamus was never one for surface show, as we commentators know to our cost.

The index date of 99 is, as usual, our chief clue, and leads us to 1999 and the death of two kings, both of whom were succeeded by their eldest sons – King Hussein of Jordan, succeeded by his son Abdullah, and King Hassan II of Morocco, succeeded by his son Mohammed VI. The Celts, though, present us with further problems, in that Nostradamus traditionally used that nomenclature to describe the French. Morocco, it is true, has French ties, following its 1904 partition of the country with Spain, and Hassan did enjoy a state visit to France just a few days before his death (foul play not suspected), but these facts still leave us none the wiser about the meaning of lines 3 and 4. Perhaps the 'casks' apply to oil, and the Western Marches to the Western Sahara, a part of the country which obsessed both Morocco and Hassan, and which he claimed on behalf of Morocco in 1975 – culminating in the Green March of 350,000 unarmed Moroccans into the territory – in an effort to mitigate public discontent against him (he had recently survived two assassination attempts)?

The United Nations finally brokered a peace deal between Morocco and the Polisario Front (who are battling for independent status for the state) in 1991, but all that is again in the balance following oil discoveries there in the last few years, and the not uncoincidental US interest in a potential West African oil base, with easy access to US Atlantic ports. *Plus ça change...*

Summary

A difficult quatrain which may refer to the Western Sahara, and to its potential in terms of oil supplies. Bad news on the surface (in the sense of territorial problems) may disguise good news underneath for the disenfranchised and often exiled Saharawi people.

POPE BENEDICT XVI

12 SEPTEMBER 2006

5 / 74

De sang Troyé naistra coeur Germanique,

Qu'il deviendra en si haulte puissance:

Hors chassera gent estrange Arabique,

Tournant l'Eglise en pristine preeminence.

A German heart is born of Trojan blood

He will wield such power

That he will chase away the foreign Arabs

Returning the Church to her immaculate
preeminence.

Well, in the light of the accession of Bavarian-born Joseph Alois Ratzinger to the papal throne on the 24th April 2005, as number 265 of an as yet unbroken line (and the first German born pope in 1,000 years, if one bars the brief 1522-23 reign of Dutch/German Adrian VI), and in the light of the newly-fledged Pope Benedict XVI's 12th September 2006 reported comments about Islam, Nostradamus appears to have hit the nail squarely on the head once again. Born at Marktl am Inn (a bare twelve uncoincidental kilometres across the river from Adolf Hitler's Austrian birthplace of Braunau am Inn), the former Cardinal Ratzinger (and archbishop of Munich and Friesing) quoted from a little-known (outside ecclesiastical circles, at least, one supposes) *Dialogue Held With A Certain Persian, The Worthy Mouterizes, In Anakara Of Galatia*: 'Show me just what Muhammad brought that was new and there you will find things only evil and inhuman, such as his command to spread by the sword the faith he preached.'

The pope was apparently highlighting Catholic theologian and non-sectarian translator of the Koran into German, Professor Adel Theodore Khoury's, commentary on the discussions held between the aforementioned Mouterizes, and Byzantine Emperor Manuel II Palaiologos, in 1391, in which Manuel made the point that warfare in the name of God (in the sense of suggesting a 'lack of reason') was contrary to God's will. Mouterizes had apparently countered by suggesting that, in Islam, God is considered to transcend so-called 'rationality', even to the extent – according to the Andalucian-born Islamic scholar Ibn Hazm

(994–1064) – 'of not being bound by his own word'. This fundamental difference (in whether God is, or is not, bound by so-called rationality) is highlighted, according to Pope Benedict, by the concept of Islamic 'forced conversion' or Jihad (anathema to modern Catholics, although not, one recalls, to their predecessors in what is now Latin America) – for this reason, just as Nostradamus infers, it may constitute the one insurmountable Chinese wall that separates the two Churches from ever fully understanding the bases of each other's doctrines.

One final (only marginally) amusing note: Sheik Abu Saqer, leader of Gaza's Jihadia Salafiya Outreach Movement, unconsciously drew together a number of Nostradamus's main quatrain images in his enraged response to the pope's words: 'The call for so-called dialogue by this little racist Pope is a Trojan Horse ... the only Christian-Muslim dialogue that is acceptable is one in which all religions agree to convert to Islam.'

Summary

Nostradamus gives us a German-born pope who galvanizes the Catholic Church against what he considers to be the more extreme and unacceptable aspects of the Islamic faith, with an emphasis on the peaceful and rational links between 'People of the Book'.

BIRTH OF AN ISLAND

Profonde argile blanche nourrit rochier,

Qui d'un abysme istra lacticineuse,

En vain troublez ne l'oseront toucher,

Ignorants être au fond terre argileuse.

A deep white clay feeds the rock

Which boils up from an abyss like milk

Needlessly afraid, the people won't dare touch it

Being ignorant of the clay in the earth's heart.

The image of a 'rock boiling up like milk' brings to mind the spontaneous creation of the island of Surtsey, near the Vestmannaeyjar (Westman Islands), off the southern coast of Iceland, on the 15th November 1963. This was a spectacular fire-and-brimstone birth, in which ash, pumice and cinders burst 1,000 feet into the sky, after more than six invisible months spent travelling to the ocean's surface. At times the ash column reached heights of 30,000 feet, and was visible from as far away as Reykjavik. Volcanic activity is commonplace beneath the surface of the oceans, so anticipating the location of any new arrival is difficult. But Nostradamus describes an environment here that is still relatively primitive – an environment possibly closed off to Western eyes. North Korea? The Indonesian Archipelago? Cuba?

SUMMARY

The birth of a new island, due to undersea volcanic activity, in an area of the world still off-limits to the West.

NEW FIRST FAMILY – PRECURSOR

Les deux contens seront unis ensemble

Quand la pluspart à Mars seront conjoinct

Le grand d'Affrique en effrayeur et tremble

Duumvirat par la classe desjoinct.

The two contenders will unite together

When most others unite with Mars

The African leader is fearful, and trembles

The dual alliance is separated by the fleet.

This seems to be a precursor to 6/24 – 2024 [New First Family], both in its use of the word *conjoint*, its concentration on dualism (*Duumvirat*), and its emphasis on the link with Mars. It seems that a false alliance is undertaken, although both sides, curiously, have made the connection in good faith. Index 6/24 has the alliance as that between a strong man and a weak, or even a male and a female leader. That said, the alliance does not, in fact, break up, but out of havoc brings appeasement – an appeasement which is, by its very nature, only a temporary alleviation of a fundamental problem.

Summary

Two great powers unite together in order to combat a global increase in internecine warfare. The alliance is a curious one, and works almost despite itself.

NEW FIRST FAMILY

2024

6 / 24

Mars et le sceptre se trouvera conjoinct,

Dessoubz Cancer calamiteuse guerre

Un peu apres sera nouveau Roi oingt,

Qui par long temps pacifiera la terre.

Mars and the sceptre are like husband and wife

Under Cancer there will be a calamitous war

Soon afterwards a new King will be anointed

Who, for a long time, will appease the earth.

Nothing is quite as it seems in this quatrain, which will come as no surprise whatsoever to scholars and amateurs of Nostradamus's conundrums. *Conjoint* does not simply mean joined, as most commentators would have it, but in Old, as opposed to Modern French, it implies a husband and wife, or an established common-law couple. In the *Compost* of Ptolemaeus, Mars is described in the following terms:

> 'Under this planet is borne theves and robbers,
> nyght walkers and quarrell pykers, bosters,
> mockers, and scoffers: and these men of Mars
> causeth warre, and murther, and batayle.'

Now here, all of a sudden, we find warlike Mars married to the virginal Sceptre, symbol of sovereignty and control, and most probably a reference to Agamemnon's famous sceptre, originally forged by Vulcan, and revered for its capacity to produce miracles.

Cancer, the crab, is famous for having bitten Hercules on the foot during his battle with the Hydra – before it had time to scuttle away to safety, however, it was duly squished by the mighty one. Juno (who had sent the hapless crustacean after Hercules in the first place) took pity on the crumpled beast, and dispatched it to heaven, where it was made one of the twelve signs of the zodiac. So are Mars, Hercules, Agamemnon's sceptre, and Cancer some kind of hidden code? This commentator's guess is that the Mars-like Agamemnon is the key, a man who sacrificed his own daughter, Iphigenia, to appease the goddess Diana and guarantee fair winds for the Greek fleet on their way to Troy. Clytemnestra, Agamemnon's adulterous wife, later slew him in his bath, and was killed, in her turn, by their son, Orestes. Just your normal, everyday, First Family, then, when one comes to think about it.

Summary

The great alliance between the two very disparate great powers, mentioned in the last quatrain, will continue. One will sacrifice the other, though, leaving one leader to appease and unify the world.

WORLDWIDE SPIRITUAL REVIVAL

Le penultiesme du surnom du prophete,
Prendra Diane pour son jour et repos
Loing vaguera par frenetique teste,
Et delivrant un grand peuple d'impos.

The last but one holder of the prophet's name

Will take Diana for his day and for his rest

He will wander far with his head in a frenzy

Delivering a great people from financial subjugation.

This quatrain is particularly interesting given its index date link with 8/28 – 2028 [Financial Meltdown – *see Nostradamus: The Complete Prophecies For The Future*]. Both deal, quite clearly, with taxes, debt, and financial crisis, but this one has a spiritual dimension as well, and forces us back to a second possible reading of 8/28, in which 'fake versions of gold and silver' become false religious icons. The Koran claims that there have been 200,000 prophets, but that only six are significant, in that they have brought in new laws and dispensations. These six are Adam, Noah, Abraham, Moses, Jesus and Muhammad. A prophet is, technically speaking, one who announces the divine will, and stems originally from Ancient Greek, although the meaning is strictly Hebrew. The Hebrews themselves recognised many prophets, and the Gautama Buddha, of course, would also come under this category, though he encapsulated the Light, rather than merely interpreting it. Nostradamus, though a scryer and seer, would certainly not have considered himself amongst their number, however.

The Roman goddess Diana's day is Monday, as she took over, amongst other things, the post of goddess of the moon from the Greek goddess Artemis. The Roman habit of filching things from the Greeks rather muddies the water where Diana is concerned, but she was also supposed to promote the union of communities, and to represent plebeians and slaves. In France Saint Lunedi was the saint associated with Mondays, and it became, in consequence, a day of rest for workers, further cementing the links in the first two lines of the quatrain. Although this does not bring us much closer to the identity of the 'last but one holder of the prophet's name', it does lead us very nicely into 2/29 – 2029 [The Sun I], which is most probably what Nostradamus intended.

Summary

Following the great financial crash of 2028, a spiritual vacuum can be detected throughout Western society. This triggers a gradual return to organised religion, and a concomitant revival in spirituality and religious practice.

THE SUN I

L'Oriental sortira de son siege,

Passer les monts Apennins, voir la Gaule:

Transpercera du ciel les eaux et neige,

Et un chacun frappera de sa gaule.

The man from the East will leave his home

And cross the Apennine Mountains,
to see France

He will pierce from the sky both the seas
and the snow

He will strike everyone with his staff.

The sun rises in the east (at least we hope so), and people are buried with their feet towards the east to show that they died in the hope of resurrection. We turn to the east when saying the Creed, and even the Greeks insisted that their cadavers should lie face upwards, and with their feet pointed towards Elysium – well away from the inferno in the west, in other words, and the sinister regions of the night. The east, then, is a powerful concept, and the place towards which we customarily look for enlightenment. All this to say that Nostradamus was most probably alluding to the sun, when he spoke of the 'man from the east', and if one reads the quatrain in that way, it is actually rather beautiful.

Another reading would judge the 'enlightenment' from the east metaphorically, as spiritual enlightenment. Here the concept of the 'staff' comes in, with its revocations of the ancient sceptre, which traditionally meant power, authority and dignity. Kings, of course, struck chosen recipients with their staff to raise them high in the realm, and to 'strike one's staff' also meant to lodge somewhere for the night, with the staff, in this instance, implying a tent staff. This brings us neatly back to the sun, and to its role in creating a suitable environment in which to grow bread – a.k.a. the 'staff of life'. So perhaps this is a prayer?

S U M M A R Y

The return to spiritual values foreseen in the last quatrain is reinforced in this hymn to the abundance of the sun, and to enlightenment.

THE SUN II

Le Sol caché eclipse par Mercure,

Ne sera mis que pour le ciel second

De Vulcan Hermes sera faicte pasture,

Sol sera veu pur, rutilant et blond.

The sun is hidden, eclipsed by Mercury

It will take second place in the sky

Hermes will be eaten by Vulcan

The sun will be seen, pure, gleaming, and fair.

This time we are dealing, not with a prayer, but with an invocation. An invocation to change. The image of Mercury is the key, with its revocations of alchemy and the transformation of base metals – we know, of course, that tiny Mercury (which is about the same size as the earth, and is the nearest planet to the sun), would not be capable of eclipsing the sun except in metaphor. So the sun is temporarily eclipsed by the power of mankind.

However, Hermes (the Greek Mercury, and in this case the symbol of the onward thrust of mankind's scientific discovery) proves to have been, quite literally, playing with fire, for he finds himself eaten, in his turn, by Vulcan, the blacksmith, whose dominion fire is (as it was of Hephaestus, with whom he is often identified). The sun, in the guise of Apollo, the great moral champion, is not so easily cowed by human actions, though, and soon shows Hephaestus who is the real boss of fire, as Milton describes in *Paradise Lost*, Book 1, from line 742 onwards:

> Sheer o'er the crystal battlements: from morn
> To noon he fell, from noon to dewy eve,
> A summer's day, and with the setting sun
> Dropt from the zenith, like a falling star.

So this is a warning, then, after the elucidatory prayer of thanks in the previous quatrain – a warning not to tinker with things greater than ourselves, and which we don't fully understand [*see* 4/28 – 2028: Discovery Of The Philosopher's Stone in *Nostradamus: The Complete Prophecies For The Future*].

Icarus, son of the talented but elusive Daedalus (himself a descendant of Hephaestus), thought that he, too, could challenge the sun, and look what happened to him. The wax on his man-made wings melted, and he fell into the Aegean Sea, part of which, as a sop, was named in his memory.

Summary

Nostradamus warns of the seductive dangers of science, at the expense of morality and right thinking. This quatrain is a paean to philosophy.

BIRTH OF A VISIONARY PAN-AFRICAN LEADER

2041

5/41

Nay souz les umbres et journée nocturne
Sera en regne et bonté souveraine
Fera renaistre son sang de l'antique urne,
Renouvellant siecle d'or pour l'aerain.

Born inside the shadows, on the very day of an eclipse

He will be sovereign in rule and goodness

He will renew his blood at the ancient urn

Restoring the golden age with bronze.

The total eclipse Nostradamus mentions in line 1 covers Angola, the Congo, Uganda, Kenya, and Somalia, so it is of a Pan-African leader that we are talking here. This reading is further strengthened by Nostradamus's use of the expression 'ancient urn' in line 3, for we now know that Africa, and in particular the geographical areas comprised within Kenya and Tanzania, was, in all probability, the cradle of human life. 'Bronze', too, has its role to play in this reading, as it was one of the earliest known alloys, and is cast on a bed of clay. The strong implication in line 4, then, is that we need to revert back to the simplicities and certainties of the past in order to be able to renew the future, and that the great African leader Nostradamus speaks of will achieve this miracle. This is a deeply optimistic quatrain, and very comforting in the light of the horrors awaiting humanity in the twenty-first century. Perhaps Africa, wisely led for a change, will be able to hold itself apart from the world conflict, and present itself as an agent for renewal and restoration, at a time of global upheaval?

SUMMARY

A great African leader is born. He will unite traditionally disparate tribes and countries, affording Africa, for only the second time in its post-colonial history, a significant influence for good on the world stage.

METEOR STRIKES AS HARBINGERS OF CHANGE

Tout aupres d'Aux, de Lectoure et Mirande,
Grande feu du ciel en trois nuits tombera:
Cause adviendra bien stupende et mirande,
Bien peu après la terre tremblera.

In the vicinity of Auch, Lectoure and Mirande

A great fire will fall from the sky over the course of three nights

A stupendous, well-aimed, and spectacular occurrence

Soon afterwards the earth will tremble and be ruffled.

Once again we find that quatrain index dates are linked in meaning across different Nostradamian *Centuries*. This time 1/46 shares the image of a 'great fire falling from the sky' with its near twin, 2/46 – 2046 [Collective Unconscious – *see Nostradamus: The Complete Prophecies For The Future*], which gives us 'fire will be seen in the sky'. This quatrain, too, uses pun and wordplay to deflect our attention from a more literal reading of the text.

Nostradamus would have known the towns of Auch, Lectoure and Mirande very well from his period of residence in Agen, in the Gers. It was there, of course, that he lost his first wife and their two children to the plague, so the place would have had mixed memories for him, of both past happiness and present grief. All the more reason then to look beyond the literal to a spiritual renewal, brought about by a physical cataclysm. For Nostradamus, the physical cataclysm would have been the death of his family, the trauma of which helped to trigger his prophetic powers. For the earth to change, and to discover its own hidden resources, Nostradamus anticipates the need for a greater – dare one say even communal – cataclysm.

SUMMARY

Some see global catastrophe as the essential trigger needed for fundamental spiritual change, while others fear the onslaught of uncertainty. Nostradamus is telling us here that good news *can* emerge from seeming catastrophe.

PEACE REIGNS OVER THE EARTH

2063

1/63

Les fléaux passés diminue le monde,
Long temps la paix terres inhabitées
Seur marchera par ciel, serre, mer, et onde:
Puis de nouveau les guerres suscitées.

With the plague over, the earth shrinks

Peace will reign for a good while

People will travel through the sky, like birds,
and by sea and wave

Before war once again is called for.

Following the terrible epidemic of 2062 [*see Nostradamus: The Complete Prophecies For The Future*], which has decimated the world population, things will return to normal. There will be peace. Travel will recommence. The word *serre* in line 3 is of particular interest here, because in Old French it means the 'talon of a bird', giving an image of people travelling through the air as if carried by a hawk – one trusts it's not invidious to remind readers, at this point, that there was no such concept as 'air travel' in Nostradamus's time. Here, he is simply taking it for granted, as if his visions had vouchsafed him a sight of the future which he accepted completely, almost as if it were an everyday matter.

The war in line 4, of course, is the global war due in 2070 [*see The Complete Prophecies For The Future*]. It is interesting to note Nostradamus's use of the word *seur*, meaning *sueur*, 'by the sweat of one's brow'. The juxtaposition of that word with *serre*, the talon of a bird, is undoubtedly intentional, and implies human, rather than godlike, will, in our mastering of the elements.

Summary

The earth's population has drastically shrunk, thanks to the worldwide epidemic of 2062. There is a period of calm and harmony in the world, possibly as a result of collective shock.

TRIUMPH OF A BENEVOLENT WORLD ORDER

2079

3/79

L'ordre fatal sempiternal par chaisne,

Viendra tourner par ordre consequent:

Du port Phocen sera rompu la chaisne:

La cite prinse, l'ennemi quant et quant.

The locked and fated eternal order of things

Will switch direction, thanks to a new order

The old Greek order will be broken

Its citadel taken, the enemy will not be accepted.

Nostradamus appears to foresee what amounts to a fundamental change in the perception of democracy ('the old Greek order'). The 'new order' (tyranny?) does not, at the very least, find easy acceptance. Phocensian Despair, of course, means desperation which terminates in victory, and stems from the days of Philip, king of Macedon, when the men of Phocis stood alone against the united might of all their enemies. As a final resort they built an enormous pyre, meaning to immolate themselves, and their women and children, upon it. Having nothing left to lose, they then threw themselves in one final, despairing act, upon the foe, and, extraordinarily, beat them off.

SUMMARY

The old world order would appear to have changed for good. Democracy is a thing of the past. There are many, however, who regret its passing. Having nothing left to lose, they ready themselves for one last-ditch attempt at a restoration of universal suffrage. Extraordinarily, and against all the odds, they are successful, igniting the beginnings of a new, more positive era.

US & CHINA SEE EYE TO EYE

2/89

Un jour seront demis les deux grands maistres,

Leur grand pouvoir se verra augmenter

La terre neufue sera en ses hauts estres,

Au sanguinaire le nombre racompté.

One day the two great leaders will become friends

Their great power will become greater

The new world will be at its highest point

The number shall be told to the red one.

It's quite encouraging to learn that after the global war of 2070 and the environmental horrors of the 2080s [*see* Mario Reading's previous *Nostradamus: The Complete Prophecies For The Future*], human nature, in the form of personal friendship, can still make a difference. The two great leaders, of course, will be those of China and the US, and the influence of the New World (North America) will have peaked. The Great Red One has already appeared in 8/80 – 2080 [Climate Change Due To Global War – *see TCPFTF*], and the telling to him of the number 'two', does not bode well. We already know about the evil inferences the number two can have numerologically, from 4/59 – 2059 [Buddhism & The Protestant Church – see *Nostradamus: The Complete Prophecies For The Future*], and the linking of this number with the 'red man' who commands the elements is far from auspicious. However, it would be churlish to dilute the glory of one of Nostradamus's few partially optimistic quatrains, due only to the sting in the tail of the last line.

SUMMARY

Their confidence shaken by the long-term fallout from the global war of 2070, the new leaders of the United States and China offer each other the hand of friendship. Peace reigns.

INDEX